A BIOGRAPHY OF

·LEVI· STRAUSS

EVERYONE WEARS HIS NAME

Sondra Henry
and Emily Taitz

A People in Focus Book

Copy 1

Dillon Press
New York

Collier Macmillan Canada
Toronto

Maxwell Macmillan International Publishing Group
New York   Oxford   Singapore   Sydney

Acknowledgments

The authors would like to acknowledge the indispensable assistance of their researchers Alice Morawetz and Laurie Nemzer, and the cooperation of Joyce Bustinduy of Levi Strauss & Co. We would also like to thank Maria Audia; Dana Francis; Tova Gazit, Judah L. Magnes Center; Jacqueline Graf, Leo Baeck Institute; Nathan M. Kaganoff, American Jewish Historical Society; John Morawetz; Irena Narell; Harriet Nathan; Annegret Ogden, Bancroft Library; Ruth Rafael, Valerie Railey, Wilkie, Farr, and Gallagher Research Libary; Harriet Rochlin; Bernice Scharlach; Dr. Norton Stern, editor, *Western Jewish History Quarterly*; Daniel Taitz; Eva Yarett.

The photographs are reproduced through the courtesy of the American Jewish Archives, Cincinnati Campus, Hebrew Union College, Jewish Institute of Religion; American Jewish Historical Society; Levi Strauss & Co.; Museum of the City of New York; New York Public Library Picture Collection; San Francisco Maritime ∙National Historical Park; Smithsonian Institution; and Western States Jewish History Center, Judah L. Magnes Museum.

Library of Congress Cataloging-in-Publication Data

Taitz, Emily.
  Everyone wears his name : a biography of Levi Strauss / by Emily Taitz and Sondra Henry.
  p.   cm. (A People in focus book)
  Bibliography: p.
  Includes index.
  ISBN 0-87518-375-1 : $11.95
  1. Strauss, Levi 1829-1902.   2. Businessmen—United States—Biography.   3. Levi Strauss and Company—History.   4. Clothing trade—United States—History.   5.Jeans (Clothing)—History.   I. Henry, Sondra.   II. Title.   III. Series.
HD9940.U4S797 1990
338.7'687'0924—dc19
[B]   87-32455
                                                                     CIP
                                                                     AC

Macmillan Publishing Company, 866 Third Avenue
New York, NY 10022

Printed in the United States of America
  3 4 5 6 7 8 9 10

Contents

Chapter One   *Passport to a new life*   5

Chapter Two   *Should'a brought pants*   22

Chapter Three   *A credit and honor to
                 the community*   32

Chapter Four   *Among our most
                 enterprising citizens*   45

Chapter Five   *I wish to make you
                 a proposition*   59

Chapter Six   *Call me Levi*   72

Chapter Seven   *My life is my business*   81

Chapter Eight   *A man with a grand character*   95

Chapter Nine   *Levi Strauss & Co.—after Levi*   102

Appendix   *The California Gold Rush*   113

Selected Bibliography   124

Index   127

Levi Strauss as a successful business owner in San Francisco.

Chapter/One

Passport to a new life

Think of "blue jeans," and the name *Levi's* probably comes to mind. Actually, *Levi* was the name of a remarkable man—Levi Strauss.

Who was Levi Strauss? People have described him as a peddler, a gold miner, a tailor, and a merchant prince. An immigrant from Germany, he was the first to make and sell the pants that became a symbol of America.

Levi's earliest customers were the miners of the California gold rush. Their clothing had to stand a great deal of rough wear. To keep up with the needs of the miners, Levi made his pants first with tough canvas, and then with the strongest denim fabric he could find.

Gradually, other workingmen and later women,

too, began wearing Levi's clothing. His pants soon earned the reputation of never wearing out or tearing at the seams. Today, the Levi's label reflects the tradition started more than a century ago by Levi Strauss & Co. It shows two horses trying to pull apart a pair of pants.

Levi's are now part of the history of the American West. People have told and retold stories about Levi Strauss and his pants until they have become legends. Many people think these stories are true, even though there are no documents to prove them.

One legend tells the story of Levi Strauss and Alkali Ike. Alkali Ike, a colorful California miner, was so big that he could never get a pair of pants to fit. When he did, he always wore them out too quickly. Then one day he bought a pair of Levi's. They fit well and did not wear out. The miner was so happy with them that he told everyone about "those pants of Levi's." Alkali Ike, says the story, made Levi Strauss famous.

Another legend tells of a family whose car was stuck in the mud. When they could not find a rope to tow it out, they used an old pair of Levi's. The car came out of the mud, and the pants did not tear.

One woman wrote that she found a pair of Levi's in a cave while she was hiking. Although dusty, they looked wearable. She brought them home, washed them, and discovered, by markings on the label, that they were eighty years old!

Many kinds of people—young and old, rich and poor—wear Levi's at some time in their lives. Once the clothes of the farmer, the miner, the cowboy, and the railroad worker, they have become more and more popular. Today, you can find them all over the world.

Did Levi Strauss really invent blue jeans? The answer to that question begins with an adventure story about a young man. More than a century ago, Levi crossed two oceans to find his fortune. He started a business empire which continues today and still bears his name.

Levi's story began in a small village in Bavaria, a land that is now the southern part of West Germany. Born on February 26, 1829, Levi (or Loeb, as he was called in German) was the youngest of six children. His oldest brothers and sister—Jacob, Jonas, Lippman, and Maila—were the children of his father's first wife, who died in 1822. Vogela and Levi were born during his father's second marriage to Rebekka Haas.

Levi's family was part of a small community of German Jews who had lived in the Bavarian village of Buttenheim for at least several generations. His father, Hirsch Strauss, made a living selling dry goods—bolts of cloth, clothing, and notions such as needles, pins, thread, and scissors.

Bavaria was a beautiful land. Its high mountains were snow-covered in winter and green in summer. Pretty villages with rows of wooden houses and peaked roofs nestled along the river banks. In the central square of each town stood a traditional church, statue, and fountains. Often there was a small Jewish quarter behind the square, with a synagogue and a house of study. Jews had roots in the land that went back as far as Roman times.

However, being a Jew in Bavaria was difficult. The new constitution of 1818 promised religious freedom to all, but promises were not always fulfilled. Levi had heard stories of riots against the Jews in other parts of Bavaria. Jews were attacked and killed in nearby cities such as Bamberg. Although this had happened ten years before Levi was born, older people still remembered it very well.

Special rules for Jewish families also added to their problems. Each Jew had to get permission from the government before he or she could marry and start a household. Since Jews were allowed to live only in one small area of the city—usually referred to as the Jewish Quarter, or the ghetto—

population growth was a problem. Non-Jewish officials usually permitted only the oldest in a family to marry and settle in that town. As a result, many young Bavarian Jews left for America.

By the time he was in his early teens, Levi had said good-bye to his half brothers, Jonas and Lippman. They had gone to seek their fortunes in the New World. Levi remained at home with his parents, his half sister Maila, and his sister Vogela.

As Levi grew older, the Buttenheim Jewish community became smaller. In addition, anti-Semitism, or hatred of Jews because of their religion or race, increased. Combined with a growing interest by Germans in their own nation and its customs, anti-Semitism led some Christians to treat their Jewish neighbors badly.

Many people saw that there was no future in Buttenheim—perhaps none in all of Bavaria—for a young Jew to make a living. If everyone in Levi's family had been healthy, the Strausses might have made the long, difficult journey across the Atlantic Ocean. But Hirsch Strauss was already sick with consumption, a lung disease for which there was no cure. The family remained in Buttenheim.

Three years later, in 1845, Levi's father died. The Strausses had little reason to remain in Bavaria, while America promised a bright future. They sold whatever they could, including their house, and packed their belongings.

In the city of Bamberg, near Buttenheim, the files still hold the application of Rebekka Strauss. She asked for permission to emigrate in 1847. That June, she received an exit visa and passports for herself and Maila, Vogela, and Levi. They were ready to sail.

The trip to America started with an overland journey by horse-drawn carriage to Hamburg or Bremerhaven, Germany's two major ports on the North Sea. Once on the ship, passengers had to be prepared for a voyage of two to three months.

The Atlantic Ocean was often stormy, and travelers suffered from seasickness. Even the first-class passengers had no fresh food or water, which made it hard to keep clean and healthy. Passengers who became sick rarely had any doctors or medicine during the voyage.

Most Jews who sailed to the United States in the mid-1800s were poor and traveled in steerage class—the worst places on the ship. Each person had only a narrow wooden bunk in which to sleep. People crowded together below decks, without windows, fresh air, or toilets.

The food offered to passengers usually consisted of lentils (dried beans) and salt pork, and

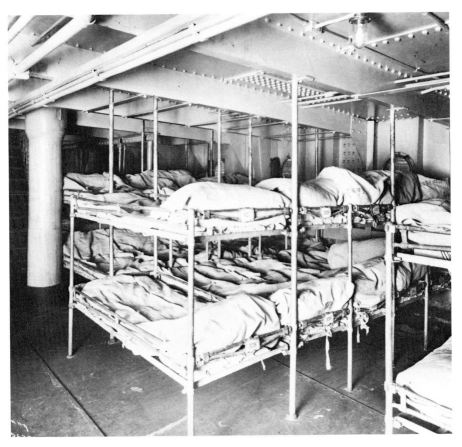

Immigrants who traveled in steerage class slept in narrow bunks during the long transatlantic voyage.

was of poor quality. Jewish travelers sometimes brought their own food with them, so they would not have to break Jewish dietary laws. However, by the end of a long voyage, it was stale if not completely spoiled.

During the Atlantic crossing, some of the passengers were weak and sick. But once they stepped onto dry land, they were eager to begin a new life.

When Levi, a young man of eighteen, first saw

Steerage-class passengers crowded the deck of this ship to catch their first glimpse of New York City and the New World.

the wharves of New York harbor in 1847, they teemed with activity. Workers loaded and unloaded crates of goods from all over the world. Fruits and vegetables, fish, sugar, coffee, and bales of cotton were stacked high. Bolts of silk from the Orient, and sturdy cloth for work clothes from France and Italy, were squeezed in between piles of lumber.

Building went on everywhere. The wooden frames of new ships stood half-finished on the

The wharves of New York harbor and the nearby streets teemed with activity.

This painting shows New York harbor about the time Levi Strauss arrived with his mother and two sisters.

wharves. Along the nearby streets, the noise of hammering filled the air. Carpenters and masons worked on houses and stores to make room for the growing population of this busy city.

Even before he left the waterfront, Levi could hear unfamiliar words of many different languages. English, Portuguese, and Spanish mixed with Swedish, German, and French. Dark-haired Italians with blue work pants hurried along next to light-skinned

Scandinavian sailors. Irish women in long, drab dresses, speaking English with a special lilt, pushed against fashionably dressed "uptown ladies" who had come to meet a passenger from a ship.

Away from the New York docks, Levi could see neat rows of narrow houses built of wood or brownstone along cobblestoned streets. Stores, buzzing with activity, sold merchandise of every description.

Goods that were not available in the stores could be found on the streets on carts piled high with odds and ends. Sometimes a tired old horse pulled a wagon. More often a man, too poor to own a shop or even a horse, pushed the cart. In between the wagons and carts, running along the streets on errands, playing, fighting, or working, were men, women, and children of all ages and descriptions.

The Strauss family became a part of this busy life. They joined many other immigrants who were struggling to fulfill their dreams in America.

Like other immigrants, Jews worked hard in this new world. Almost all had been poor in Europe. Some had used the last of their funds to cross the ocean. When they reached New York, they searched out relatives or *landsmen*—people who once lived in their hometown—who might help them.

Levi's brothers, Jonas and Lippman (now called Louis), were already settled in New York by 1847. Like their father, they earned a living in the dry goods business. Their stepmother, Rebekka, and the three grown Strauss children went directly to them when they arrived.

In lower New York, the southern part of the island of Manhattan, several streets were inhabited by Jews. A few of these immigrants had small stores, but most were still too poor even to rent a shop. Like so many others, the recent arrivals sold goods from a cart or carried them on their backs.

Most Jewish businesses were located on Chatham Square and Houston, Division, and Grand streets. This area was sometimes referred to as the Hebrew Market.

One Jewish immigrant, who arrived at the same time as Levi Strauss, remembered lower New York as "a large shop where everyone buys or sells, cheats or is cheated....On that first day, I longed to be away."

In spite of first impressions like these, many German Jews remained in New York. Others went further inland—usually to the south and west—searching for new business opportunities.

Levi's sister, Vogela, now known by her American name, Fanny, soon married David Stern,

Jewish immigrants sold goods from carts on Hester Street in New York.

another immigrant. After a few years, the couple settled in Saint Louis, Missouri.

Maila, called Mary in America, married William Sahlein, an uncle. At first William worked as a tailor in New York City. Eventually, they also left New York to seek their fortunes in the American West.

By 1848, Jonas Strauss had opened up his own small dry goods store at 203-1/2 Division Street

in New York City, and worked with his brother
Louis. With Louis and Jonas to guide him, Levi
now began to learn the business.

Levi probably worked for his brothers when
he first came to New York. He selected goods with
their help, listened to their advice, and learned the
skills of buying and selling. Then, when he was
nineteen years old, he traveled to Kentucky—still a
wild frontier state in 1848—and remained there for
some time, selling dry goods and notions. As a peddler, Levi was following an American tradition.

The original peddlers in the American frontier lands were "yankees" from New England. They
carried items such as pins, needles, hooks and
eyes, scissors, razors, combs, buttons, cotton goods,
lace, and perfume. These traveling salesmen
trudged along from town to town, bringing necessary goods to isolated rural families. Along with
their needles and thread, they also brought the
news and gossip of the surrounding areas.

At first, peddlers carried packs on their backs
or sometimes even trunks. When they could save
enough money, they purchased a horse and cart.
Then they could bring along many more things,
such as bolts of cloth or ready-made clothing.

By the mid-1830s German Jews, many from
Bavaria, slowly replaced the original Yankee ped-

dlers. Peddling presented an opportunity for new immigrants to America who might have had difficulty finding other jobs. It gave them a chance to learn the language and the customs of their new country. In addition, they needed only a small amount of money for their stock. Eight or ten dollars was enough to make a peddler's pack bulge with merchandise. It was not unusual for a peddler to walk as far as ten miles in order to sell a few dollars worth of notions.

Before he could go to Kentucky, Levi first had to select his merchandise. Entering the giant warehouse in New York where all the peddlers' supplies were available was both exciting and bewildering. Imagine someone who lived in a busy city such as New York trying to choose just the right items to sell to the Kentucky farmers and woodsmen! There was a huge selection of colored yarns and threads, pins and needles arranged in rows on sheets of paper, yards of shiny ribbon, starched white handkerchiefs, and much more. In fact, the peddler would carry a small general store on his back.

For Levi to succeed as a peddler, he had to be young and strong, able to carry a pack or trunk weighing as much as 100 pounds. He could not fear being alone, getting lost, or meeting robbers or wild animals. From time to time, townspeople

Many Jewish peddlers carried their goods in small trunks, packs, or satchels.

heard stories about a peddler who was murdered on the road.

Many peddlers slept in barns and ate food given to them by farm families. For twenty-five cents they got supper, a bed, and breakfast at a local farmhouse. If they could afford more, they slept at a tavern or an inn. Starting out in this way, Levi was no different than hundreds of Bavarian Jews who walked the roads of Kentucky, slowly learning English and becoming Americans.

Jews eventually gave up peddling and settled down. For a peddler with a horse and wagon, sometimes the decision to stop traveling was not his own. When his horse died, or was too weak to continue, the peddler stopped and opened a store. Many famous department store owners such as Adam Gimbel, Marshall Field, and Benjamin Altman began as peddlers and later became rich merchants.

After several years, Levi Strauss left Kentucky. Now in his early twenties, the dark-eyed, solemn young man could not know that this decision marked the beginning of a truly American success story. His dreams would bring him from one end of the country to the other and make his name a household word in every city in his adopted land.

Chapter/Two

Should'a brought pants

"Gold! Gold! Gold!"

That was the cry that went up at Sutter's Mill in the northern part of California territory. In January 1848, less than a year after Levi Strauss had arrived in the United States, gold was discovered in California. The news spread first by word of mouth and then through newspapers and letters from one person to another, from one family to another, until everyone in California knew.

Gold had been discovered! And there was reason to believe that much more of it could be found in the rocks and stones and streams which had just become United States territory at the end of the Mexican War. Anyone brave, or adventurous, or hard-working enough, could go and find it.

From California, the news traveled south in ships: through the Pacific Ocean, around Cape Horn—the southernmost tip of South America—and north through the Atlantic Ocean to the United States ports of Norfolk, Philadelphia, New York, and Boston. From there it spread inland to new frontier states such as Missouri, Ohio, and Kentucky, where Levi Strauss lived and worked. All kinds of people began making their way to California to claim their share of the riches.

The long and dangerous ocean voyage around the Horn, taking as long as five months, was one way of traveling from the East to the West. Another choice was to travel by smaller ships, called steamers, down the eastern coast of North America to Panama or Nicaragua. These were the two narrowest overland crossings between the Atlantic and Pacific oceans. In Panama the travelers would leave the steamer and make their way up the Chagres River. From there, they would begin an overland trek by foot or mule, across the narrow isthmus to the town of Panama, carrying their belongings with them. When they reached the Pacific Ocean, they boarded another steamer for the voyage to San Francisco.

A third way to reach the West Coast was overland by wagon train. About half of the travelers came this way. They joined a group of pioneers who gathered in central cities such as Saint Louis, Missouri, and traveled together in covered wagons. Usually leaving in early May, when the snows of the Rocky Mountains had melted, they crossed deserts, mountains, and rivers. They risked disease and attacks by native Americans whose lands they crossed. Another danger was the breakdown of the wagons or the animals, which might cause long delays. Many wagon trains never reached their destinations.

Since the first pioneers were mainly gold seekers, very few females were among them. But within a few years women, too, were coming west. Advertisements such as the one posted in Boston by the California Emigration Society promised passage on a ship with "good physicians, both male and female." "Females are getting almost as good wages as males," said this same poster, which offered to find housing and jobs for anyone who came.

Fanny and David Stern, Levi Strauss's sister and brother-in-law, were among the people who heard about the gold rush. From Saint Louis, they traveled overland to California. Like many of the Bavarian Jews who came at that time, David and Fanny brought merchandise—mostly dry goods— and began a small business in San Francisco.

EMIGRATION TO CALIFORNIA !

Do you want to go to California ? If so, go and join the Company who intend going out the middle of March, or 1st of April next, under the charge of the California Emigration Society, in a first-rate Clipper Ship. The Society agreeing to find places for all those who wish it upon their arrival in San Francisco. The voyage will probably be made in a few months.— Price of passage will be in the vicinity of

ONE HUNDRED DOLLARS !

CHILDREN IN PROPORTION.

A number of families have already engaged passage. A suitable Female Nurse has been provided, who will take charge of Young Ladies and Children. Good Physicians, both male and female go in the Ship. It is hoped a large number of females will go, as Females are getting almost as good wages as males.

FEMALE NURSES get 25 dollars per week and board. SCHOOL TEACHERS 100 dollars per month. GARDNERS 60 dollars per month and board. LABORERS 4 to 5 dollars per day. BRICKLAYERS 6 dollars per day. HOUSEKEEPERS 40 dollars per month. FARMERS 5 dollars per day. SHOEMAKERS 4 dollars per day. Men and Women COOKS 40 to 60 dollars per month and board. MINERS are making from 3 to 12 dollars per day. FEMALE SERVANTS 30 to 50 dollars per month and board. Washing 3 dollars per dozen. MASONS 6 dollars per day. CARPENTERS 5 dollars per day. ENGINEERS 100 dollars per month, and as the quartz Crushing Mills are getting into operation all through the country, Engineers are very scarce. BLACKSMITHS 90 and 100 dollars per month and board.

The above prices are copied from late papers printed in San Francisco, which can be seen at my office. Having views of some 30 Cities throughout the State of California, I shall be happy to see all who will call at the office of the Society, 28 JOY'S BUILDING, WASHINGTON ST., BOSTON, and examine them. Parties residing out of the City, by enclosing a stamp and sending to the office, will receive a circular giving all the particulars of the voyage.

As Agents are wanted in every town and city of the New England States, Postmasters or Merchants acting as such will be allowed a certain commission on every person they get to join the Company. Good reference required. For further particulars correspond or call at the

SOCIETY'S OFFICE,

28 Joy's Building, Washington St., Boston, Mass.

Propeller Job Press, 143 Washington Street. Boston

This California Emigration Society poster advertised passage on a ship to California for one hundred dollars. It also gave information about wages for different jobs in California.

Levi decided to join his sister Fanny and her family, and begin the western branch of the Strauss business. But in order to get to San Francisco, he first had to endure another stormy sea voyage. The trip around South America, through the Strait of Magellan, was the most dependable means of travel and transport in those early years, but it was extremely difficult.

One traveler, writing about a similar voyage to California, said: "Nobody can imagine how an immigrant feels during a storm. The wind is whipping the water against the ship which sometimes sounds like the explosion of a bomb and we are almost waiting for the whole thing to burst."

Unlike many other Jews who came to California directly from Bavaria during that period, Levi had already lived in America. From letters and newspapers in New York, and his own experiences in Kentucky, he knew a little of the shortages in this faraway territory. He had heard that apples sold for fifty cents in California—at least ten times the East Coast price—and eggs cost a dollar each, instead of a nickel. A simple wagon worth $15 in the East sold for $100 or more on the West Coast.

Traveling to San Francisco, the gateway to the gold mines, it seemed to Levi that the whole world had caught "gold fever." In 1853, five years after

that first discovery, men were still coming to the
mines with dreams of "rivers running with gold."
Most had never even used a pick and shovel. They
were farmers, lawyers, preachers, and shopkeepers
who staked their claims in the California mountains. Many had no knowledge of the climate or
the difficult conditions they would find there.
Mostly young, unmarried men from all over the
world, they passed through San Francisco and
made their way to the "diggings." Only a small
number actually found gold, but they did build a
new state and new cities.

San Francisco had been called Yerba Buena
under Mexican rule. Before the discovery of gold,
it was a small, sleepy outpost of a few hundred
people and a scattering of adobe houses. The first
settlers who came in 1848 set up tents and shacks
for temporary shelter. Then, "knock-down" frame
houses—manufactured in eastern cities and shipped
to California—replaced the tents. But many fires
destroyed these early wooden homes.

By 1851, the number of ships abandoned in
San Francisco's harbor had grown to more than
700. Like the thousands of other men who had left
businesses and stores, or walked out of print shops
and newspaper offices, the sailors simply ran off to
pan for gold. They sometimes left their ships still

San Francisco in 1852, a year before Levi Strauss sailed into the harbor.

filled with cargo. Since the city's officials found it too difficult to clear the harbor of these ships, they allowed them to sink into the mud and built the wharves right over them.

Gradually, wooden walkways covered the mud pathways leading from the docks. They were lined with dance halls, saloons, and gambling casinos which offered male visitors an evening of entertainment. Miners came to San Francisco only long enough to rest, get drunk, and buy new supplies before returning to the diggings.

By 1850, San Francisco's population had swelled to 25,000, and California had become a U.S. state. Almost overnight, the city spread inland. People built boarding houses, hotels, shops, and warehouses. By 1853, when Levi Strauss's ship finally steamed into San Francisco Bay, the city had 70,000 people.

Levi, a young man of twenty-four, stood proudly at five feet six inches. Dark-complexioned and dark-haired, he dressed formally in a black waistcoat. His clothing was somewhat like the style that had been popular among the Jews of Bavaria. An early photograph shows him with a dark beard shaped into the fashionable muttonchop whiskers of that time.

San Francisco needed and welcomed businessmen such as Levi. Attracted by the promise of new opportunity and adventures, merchants had begun to settle in the city with their families by the early 1850s. Now there were homes and houses of worship. One of these homes belonged to the Sterns, Levi Strauss's family.

Like his brother-in-law David Stern, Levi came with much-needed merchandise to sell: needles, thread, scissors, and other sewing supplies, as well as rolls of canvas. All had been supplied by his brothers in the East, who were now in larger quarters at 165 Houston Street, New York City.

It is in San Francisco that the Levi legend really begins. According to one story, eager merchants rowed out to meet Levi's ship even before it docked and quickly bought up most of his goods. Before he set foot in San Francisco, Levi sold everything except the canvas.

People still tell stories about that leftover roll of canvas. When he offered the last of his merchandise for sale, Levi was told: "Should'a brought pants. Pants don't wear worth a hoot in the diggin's."

After hearing this remark, Levi brought his brown canvas to a tailor and had his first pair of work pants made. Later, the demand for Levi's sturdy pants was so great that he could not get enough cloth. When a shipment from his brothers in New York did not arrive on time, says one story, he even used sails from the abandoned ships in the harbor, and canvas from covered wagons that had made the overland trip to the West!

Another legend says that Levi, after selling out his first shipment, took to the gold fields himself, and tried his hand at digging for gold. Historians say he did not.

An ambitious man, Levi Strauss saw in the

fast-growing state of California a chance to build a new life. The people needed everything from food and clothes to services of all kinds. A hard-working businessman, no matter what his religion or background, could make his fortune outside the gold fields.

In California all types of people had an equal chance to succeed. Anti-Semitism was not common among Californians, and few cared about titles or past reputations. Real accomplishments counted for more than fine clothes and fine manners.

Levi Strauss accepted this new standard and wasted no time in getting started. Shortly after his arrival and his first selling success, he arranged to pay the city business-license fee. Just $100 in quarterly installments gave him the right to join David Stern in business. Soon they had their own shop.

Chapter/Three

A credit and honor to the community

Levi Strauss and David Stern followed the example of many other merchants when they set up a store in San Francisco. Fellow Jews from Germany such as Abraham Haas, Adolph Sutro, Aaron Fleishhacker, and the Steinhart brothers had already built businesses there. They set good examples for Levi and David in their first struggles to establish themselves.

The first building that the two young brothers-in-law found for their small dry-goods business was close to the docks. Built on pilings to avoid flooding during high tide, it stood at the end of the Sacramento Street wharf.

Everything happened at the waterfront in San Francisco. By 1853 the city boasted twenty-three

This early photograph shows one of the many wharves leading to the San Francisco harbor. Here, goods were loaded, unloaded, and stored.

wharves. Laborers loaded and unloaded goods there, and merchants bought and sold them.

Shops lined the wooden walkways leading to the wharves. Newcomers pitched their tents in the mud set back from the harbor. If they wanted to visit a saloon, there were 399 of them to choose from. The next day they bought their supplies in one of the 117 dry-goods stores, and went north to the gold fields.

In the early 1850s San Francisco was an isolated city that depended on ships. Ships brought
in almost every article of clothing, tool, and uten-
sil, as well as much of the city's food and drink.
San Francisco's merchants read the newspaper, the
Daily Alta California, which announced the arrival
of all vessels and listed their cargos and passengers.
When a cargo ship arrived, no matter how small,
businesspeople in town knew about it.

Importing goods by ship was expensive and
risky and took a long time. While a letter reached
California from New York in three weeks, goods
could take months to arrive. Mail was sent by ship
to Panama, overland across the isthmus, and then
by steamer to New York on the Pacific Steamship
Mail Lines. Clothing and fabrics were much heav-
ier and had to be transported by large clipper ships
around the Horn.

Even Levi and David, who had a direct supply
from their family in New York, had problems
keeping their shop well stocked. They, too, waited
for other ships to arrive, and then rushed to the
auctions to purchase what they could.

Storms at sea, delays at other ports along the
way, and a variety of other problems made it
impossible to predict exactly when a ship would
arrive in port. Some even sank in the stormy

waves of the Strait of Magellan and never arrived with their valuable cargo.

Young boys, sometimes no more than eleven or twelve years old, were hired as lookouts to watch for ships approaching the harbor. They were posted on the hills with spyglasses, where they watched for a glimpse of white sails far out in San Francisco Bay. As soon as they saw a ship, they would run to tell the merchants. If the weather was clear, Levi would have a full day's notice.

What would the clipper ship be carrying? If it carried a supply of blankets, then the price for blankets already in the city's shops would drop from forty dollars to perhaps twenty dollars or less. The same situation applied to needles and thread, men's shirts, or bolts of fabric. Lowering the price meant store owners had at least some chance to sell, and making even a very small profit was better than losing money.

Starting a new business required a great deal of hard work. Levi and David worked—sometimes day and night. With store blankets to cushion the damp wood, on some nights they slept on the floor of their cluttered shop. They did it only when a ship was scheduled to arrive from the East. Then they had to be there, ready for whatever might come.

David Stern marked down the goods in their

In the 1850s, sailing ships filled San Francisco's harbor. Levi Strauss, and the city itself, depended on ships for essential supplies.

shop and waited for the customers to come looking for bargains. Meanwhile, Levi hurried out to the ship to attend the auction at which the goods were sold. For David and Levi, sleeping in their store and being the first to arrive at the ship could mean the difference between a month's profit or a month's loss.

The auctions were crowded with people who were eager to buy for any price. Tin plates and cups, which cost a few cents in the East, might be worth several dollars to a miner going off to pan gold. A penny-pack of needles sold for twenty-five cents in San Francisco. Merchants bid as high as they could for valuable items such as wagons, wheels, tools, work clothes, and liquor.

Levi rarely knew what he was about to purchase until he arrived at the auction. It could be work clothes, made with fabric imported from Nîmes, a city in France. This strong material was called *serge de Nîmes* in French. It was shortened to *denim* in English as early as 1695. Miners preferred denim clothes because they were strong and long wearing.

Levi considered himself lucky to obtain a shipment of denim work pants, or even just the fabric, at one of these auctions. He also bid for men's work shirts, canvas, blankets, hats, and notions to sell at the shop along with the work pants. If a ship arrived later than expected, or if there was a shortage of any item, Levi and David might sell out their stock completely before the day was over.

Besides attending auctions and working in the store, Levi Strauss also traveled to northern California mining towns to sell dry goods to local merchants and shops. Levi followed the path of mining camps which grew up along the Sierra Nevada mountain chain. Some of these mining camps had funny names such as Bedbug, Groundhog's Glory, Henpeck City, and Rough and Ready. They were named by the miners themselves, perhaps based on their own experiences when they first arrived.

Conditions in the mining camps were difficult, and work was hard. The miner first needed a pick and shovel to clear off two feet of earth. Then he would place a shovelful of dirt in a tin pan, carry it to a nearby stream or river, stir up the dirt in water, and heave out the stones. This process continued until, after many washings, only gold and heavy minerals were left. If a miner was lucky, there would be from one to five dollars worth of gold in his pan. Using this time-consuming method, it often took a full day to get two spoonfuls of gold.

Miners had to work in all kinds of weather. One miner described how his eyes became bloodshot and his hands swollen in the burning heat. Others were caught in storms or cold.

It was hard to find decent food, or even a tent to sleep in. Ordinary provisions such as potatoes and eggs were much more expensive in the camps than they were in San Francisco. Miners and merchants were sometimes killed in their sleep and robbed of precious supplies as well as gold.

The first peddlers who came to the diggings

A Chinese miner panning for gold.

were welcomed for the boots, work pants, shovels, and mining tools that they brought. However, they soon found that it was too difficult to travel in the rugged mountains with a heavy pack, walking from one mining camp to another. As soon as they could afford a horse and wagon, and were able to carry larger amounts, they sold their supplies to store owners who had opened shops near the mines.

In his earliest years, Levi, an ambitious young salesperson, visited towns such as Placerville, Maryville, Murphys, Mariposa, Vallecito, Eureka, and Downieville. Sometimes these small towns consisted of not much more than a few bars, a boarding house, the local dry-goods store, and a small Chinese section where new immigrants from China gathered. In addition to the mining, the Chinese worked for pennies doing anything the other men could not or would not do.

At first, Levi Strauss and David Stern took care of the needs of miners. Then, as the population changed, the partners began to serve families, too. They continued to supply the many small merchants in mining outposts to the north and east of San Francisco, sending additional goods such as women's and children's clothing to their new customers. Small shopkeepers came to trust Levi and to depend on his honesty and reliability.

The Strauss business steadily grew, along with the city of San Francisco. Early in 1853, when Levi first arrived, only a few lights had been installed to light up San Francisco's streets. By the end of the year, most of the streets had oil lamps. By this time the city also had five theaters. They featured plays and musical entertainment that was more tasteful than the loud music of the gambling houses and saloons.

Solid citizens such as Levi Strauss and the Sterns disapproved of gambling houses and saloons. Unmarried men went to have a good time there, and drunkenness and violence were encouraged.

Many San Franciscans believed that more women would make California a less violent place. The local newspaper claimed that the city's more peaceful Sundays were due "to the fact that we have many more families amongst us. The increase in the number of ladies," it said, "is surely creating that revolution which the virtuous and amiable of the sex always produces."

Still, citizens complained about violence almost daily. In 1853, the year that Levi arrived, 1,200 murders had been recorded in San Francisco alone, and rumors of another 2,400 had spread through the city.

"Lawlessness" was the complaint of those

times. "Crimes increase and punishment is evaded, men robbed and murdered, houses and stores plundered, and the city again and again set on fire," reported the newspapers. Editorial writers urged a change in the law so that troublemakers could be brought to justice quickly. But making new rules took a long time.

To stop the killing and fighting, men formed vigilante committees. These committees planned to bring the lawbreakers to justice without having to wait for the courts. Just down the street from Levi and David's business, a vigilante committee set up its headquarters in 1856. The vigilantes hanged two men there, in full view of the store.

Although some Jews did favor the vigilantes, law-abiding Jewish citizens rarely got involved with them. They were more concerned with attempts by the state legislature to pass a Sunday closing law. This law would make it illegal to keep a shop or other business open on Sundays. If it passed, Jews who followed Jewish Law carefully and did not work on Saturdays (the Jewish Sabbath) would be forced to stay closed for two days every week.

Even Jews who did not observe the Sabbath worried that this might be the beginning of anti-Jewish laws in America. Such rules against Jews had been common throughout Europe. Many of

San Francisco's Jewish citizens, including Levi Strauss, could still remember them.

Jews finally did support the Sunday closing law, which was passed in 1858. They understood that by making all businesses close on one day, gambling casinos and saloons would also have to close. These less desirable businesses had originally been the main target of the law.

Levi Strauss did not observe the Jewish Sabbath. He worked six long days a week, from Monday through Saturday. The partners opened up their store at 6:00 A.M. and closed at 6:00 P.M. During those first years, young Levi had little time for any other activity but business.

In the spring of 1853, shortly after Levi Strauss's arrival, Jews had begun to collect money to build a synagogue of their own. Within a year, the new building was completed. Levi, although not as devoted a member as David Stern, joined and supported the synagogue, Temple Emanu-el. Later in his life, he became one of its most prominent members.

Along with the growing number of families in San Francisco, the Jewish community also grew. However, there continued to be fewer women than men. This may help explain why Levi Strauss, though young and very eligible by the standards of

the day, never married. Because he lived with his
sister Fanny, his brother-in-law David Stern, and
their children, Henry, Jacob, and Caroline, Levi
enjoyed the comforts of home and a close family.

As for business, it had never been better. By
1858, Levi Strauss had become the head of the
firm, and a successful businessperson. Imports
from France and Germany filled the Levi Strauss
& Co. catalog. Irish linen, Belgian lace, and Italian
shawls tempted Levi's customers.

In 1861, an enthusiastic observer, commenting
on the success of San Francisco's Jews, wrote: "On
a first arrival in our city, it becomes a matter of
astonishment to all who see the large number of
mercantile houses conducted by Israelites....Every
line of business is engaged in by them, with credit
to themselves and honor to the community." Levi
Strauss was one of these "Israelites," as Jews were
politely called at that time.

On February 1, 1861, the S.S. *California* sailed
east with a shipment of gold to pay New York sup-
pliers. Exactly $59,732.24 worth of that gold be-
longed to Levi Strauss & Co.

Chapter/Four

Among our most enterprising citizens

By 1861, Levi Strauss had shown that he had the best business sense in the family. During the years of the Civil War, he established himself even more firmly at the head of a growing business. Although David Stern was the senior partner and founder, Levi was without question "the boss."

Other family members also helped the business grow. William Sahlein, Levi's brother-in-law, had become a partner in San Francisco. Nathan Strauss, Levi's nephew from New York, would soon join them.

Most of the sales and some manufacturing was done by the company's western branch. In New York, Jonas and Louis Strauss ran the eastern branch of the company. They manufactured some

Levi Strauss during the 1860s, wearing his black topcoat and silk top hat.

goods, imported others, and shipped a steady supply to the West Coast. But it was Levi who gave his name to the company, and made the important decisions.

The days when miners came in and paid a dollar for a pair of Levi's canvas pants were past. Now Levi headed a company that sold clothing and supplies to stores and salespeople throughout the West. Its stock included bed linen, blankets, sweaters, socks, underwear, women's clothing, and work clothes. These were all made by other companies, and sold by Levi Strauss & Co. as wholesale goods.

Levi's work pants were still one of the most well-known items in his catalog. By this time, though, they were not made from canvas, but from imported French denim.

The denim came in large bolts, either in natural white, called "duck," or dyed a deep indigo blue. Levi Strauss & Co. distributed the fabric to individual tailors. They cut and sewed it into pants in their own homes.

Levi called these pants "waist high overalls." He preferred this name to the common word: *jeans*. At the time *jeans* referred to a cheap type of work pants made of cotton imported from Genoa, Italy. The French word for Genoa—*Gênes*—became the name for the pants themselves.

Like miners throughout the West, these miners at the LaGrange mine wore work pants made by Levi Strauss & Co.

Once Levi had gone on the road to sell his merchandise. Now he had salespeople to do this work, and a catalog to advertise a wide variety of goods. Levi remained in San Francisco to supervise and organize the company.

When the famed Pony Express began its route in 1860, sending mail between the San Francisco and New York branches of the business became easier. The Pony Express was a delivery service that used fast horses in relays to bring mail across the western United States. The express service took nine days from Sacramento, California, to Saint Joseph, Missouri. From there, the mail was picked up by railroad and sent on to New York.

Once the Pony Express began, Levi could send a letter to Jonas and Louis and know that it would be delivered in New York in two weeks. The following year, when the Pacific Telegraph linked the East to the West in Salt Lake City, Utah, mail service by the Pony Express ended. Now messages could be sent across the continent almost instantly. Businesses such as Levi's, which depended on supplies from the East, could now place an order within hours rather than weeks.

In addition, Californians eagerly awaited the railroad that would connect the West with the rest of the United States. A transcontinental railroad would bring letters, merchandise, and even people from New York to San Francisco in only one week's time. But the Civil War delayed its completion.

Since California had been admitted to the Union as a "free" rather than "slave" state, slavery had never been an issue for Californians. Most state residents sided with the Union—the North—and supported President Lincoln. Jews were especially loyal to the president and the federal government, because they appreciated the freedom they had in their new country. When Abraham Lincoln was assassinated, special memorial services were held in synagogues throughout the state.

In spite of the loyalty of California's citizens to the Union cause, the Union Army did not use many western soldiers. There were some volunteers, but it was too expensive to send a large number of troops from the Pacific coast to battlefields in the East. For this reason, California was not affected by the high death tolls that other states suffered.

During the Civil War, goods arriving in San Francisco cost even more than they had before. The war made trading complicated and risky. Both northern and southern armies attacked merchant vessels in an attempt to destroy the other side's commerce. Because of a Union blockade, trade in cotton was especially difficult, since it arrived by ship from the South.

While the war lasted, Levi Strauss sometimes had to wait for months before a shipment came through from New York with supplies for the company. Under these conditions, Levi had trouble filling orders. Both his local customers, as well as storekeepers throughout northern California and Nevada, had grown to depend on him.

In spite of these problems, Levi never smuggled illegal cotton and other supplies from the South. A few other merchants did engage in smuggling, and they were condemned by the government.

California's merchants and shippers supplied a growing number of state residents, and also shipped goods to the East to aid in the war effort. The Union desperately needed California wool, food products, and especially gold to pay for supplies for its army. Throughout the war, Levi managed to keep his business going without southern cotton.

Finally, in spring 1865, the Civil War ended. Peace between the North and the South brought increased growth to business and industry throughout the country. In the West, many companies benefitted from the trade that began to flow freely between the southern and northern states.

The gold rush had produced more than $800 million worth of gold during the first ten years. The men who had made fortunes at that time later built beautiful homes which they filled with fine furniture. San Francisco, a city of shacks and tents only two decades before, now had houses that rivaled the mansions of Europe.

Levi Strauss shared in and contributed to the growth of San Francisco as a commercial and industrial capital. In 1865 Levi Strauss & Co. purchased a piece of real estate known in San Francisco as the Oriental Hotel. The valuable old property was located in the center of town, at the intersection of Market, Bush, and Sansome streets.

Shortly after buying the hotel, Levi, David Stern, and William Sahlein began discussing the idea of building their own headquarters. It was time for the company to expand. Like the old shop on Sacramento Street, their new headquarters had to be well located and not too far from the wharves. But this time they had more money to spend, and could afford to select a site more carefully. Soon work began on the new store, which was built on solid ground instead of wooden pilings over the mud. Inside, the four-story building had offices, shipping rooms, and departments for all types of dry goods.

In a city that had suffered from so many fires, the choice of building materials was considered important. Well before Levi had come to California, six city-wide fires had destroyed large parts of San Francisco. As a result, the new headquarters was built from brick and other materials that were strong and fireproof.

Neither Levi nor his partners expected the test to come as soon as it did. This time it was not a fire, but an earthquake—another earthquake!

The first earthquake Levi had ever felt took place on October 8, 1865. This had been a new experience for thirty-six-year-old Levi. Almost exactly three years later, on October 21, 1868, it happened again.

When the earth began to shake, people ran into the street. It was safer to be out in the open, away from any structure that might collapse. That first 1868 quake lasted only a few seconds. It was followed about an hour later by a second, more violent one. As the *Daily Alta California* described it: "When the great shock culminated, a stampede from every building in the city took place. Hundreds of horses on the streets, startled by the rush of people, took fright and ran away, adding to the danger and excitement of the moment."

When it ended, San Franciscans called it the worst earthquake in living memory. The quake had damaged some of the major buildings in the downtown area. A few were partially destroyed.

Rushing downtown to check the damage, Levi, David, and William were shocked. Although their new building was still standing, it showed signs of considerable damage. Outside, a large crack ran across the building's front side. "Levi Strauss & Co.'s building, erected but a few months," reported the newspapers, "is cracked through and through."

Inside, there was dust and dirt everywhere. The new offices, which had been so elegant and orderly, were a shambles. Stacks of clothing that had been neatly folded were shaken from the shelves and strewn about on the floor. Disorderly piles of goods were covered with crumbled plaster which had come loose from the walls and ceiling. Still, the damage could have been far worse, and none of the company's employees was injured or killed. In all of San Francisco, four people were killed, and many others suffered serious injuries.

Employees took the merchandise from Levi Strauss & Co. and cleaned, folded, and put it away. Levi, David, and William began to plan for a new headquarters building on Battery Street. Along with other San Franciscans, Levi returned to his normal and comfortable routines at work and at home.

Levi Strauss lived on Powell Street with Fanny and David Stern. By this time the Sterns had eight children. Fanny, with the help of several servants, kept the large household running smoothly.

Each morning, formally dressed in a black suit and a silk black stovepipe hat, Levi left the house on Powell Street and walked to work. By 10:00 A.M. he was always in his office.

Levi Strauss enjoyed considerable respect and had a high status in the community. His success in business led to membership in civic-minded groups such as the Eureka Benevolent Society. This was a Jewish charitable organization which helped orphans, widows, and needy Jews in the San Francisco area. One of its earliest projects was to raise money, together with Temple Emanu-el, to purchase land for a cemetery for the growing Jewish community.

The cornerstone for a synagogue had been laid in 1864. Both Levi Strauss and his sisters' families contributed money to the new Sutter Street building, considered one of the most beautiful buildings in San Francisco. This elegant temple, topped with two graceful, domed towers, survived both earthquakes with no damage.

Although Levi Strauss did not attend Temple Emanu-el's services regularly, he did contribute money to the synagogue. Each year, Levi Strauss, along with Louis Sloss, another Bavarian Jew, donated a real gold medal to the temple. It was presented to the child who had earned the highest grades in the Sabbath school.

Levi Strauss had no children of his own, but was very fond of his nieces and nephews. He felt closest to Fanny's five sons. After her son Henry died, the other four—Jacob, Sigmund, Louis, and Abraham—became even more important to him. One day they would inherit the family's business.

The first Sutter Street building of Congregation Emanu-el in San Francisco.

Levi took an active interest in his nephews' education, and later, in their careers and their marriages. He was an important member of the Stern family. The children respected their uncle, listened to his advice, and were eager to please him.

Beyond his family, he became acquainted with many other people through religious, social, and civic activities. On the High Holidays—the Jewish New Year and Day of Atonement—he attended prayer services with the growing membership of Temple Emanu-el. Like Levi, many of these San Franciscans were successful merchants. Some rode to the synagogue in fancy coaches with uniformed drivers.

When he was not working, Levi could take advantage of San Francisco's cultural events. The riches of the gold rush had helped the cultural growth of San Francisco. Libraries, art galleries, theaters, concert halls, and social and literary clubs gave people a choice of many things to do. Although it was a new city, at one time San Francisco had more newspapers than London.

In 1869, when the honorary committee of the California Immigrant Union was founded, Levi was invited to become a member. One of the purposes of this group was to promote products from California. The honorary committee also encouraged immigration from Europe and the East Coast of the United States. The committee shared in the excitement when the transcontinental railroad officially opened on May 10, 1869.

The Union Pacific Railroad joined the Central Pacific at Promontory Summit, Utah. This landmark event, which finally joined the East and the West, would change the future and the face of America. Now people and goods could come by train straight across the country to California. No longer did they have to take the long sea route around Cape Horn, or the dangerous trek across the isthmus of Panama.

As Levi became more successful, his outside activities continued to grow. However, his work came first in his life, and his business offered him his greatest challenges.

Because Levi Strauss was so committed to his company, he would not let an opportunity pass that might help the business expand. Just such an opportunity came in the early 1870s. It arrived in the form of a letter from Jacob Davis, a customer in neighboring Nevada. Mr. Davis had an interesting proposal.

Chapter/Five

I wish to make you a proposition

Jacob Davis was a Jewish tailor who had come to the United States from Riga, Latvia, a city on the Baltic Sea in what is now the Soviet Union. Born in 1831, just two years after Levi Strauss, he had come to New York at about the same time. But unlike Levi Strauss, his life had not been very successful.

Before Jacob Davis arrived in California in 1856, he had worked as a tailor in many places. Jacob had tried many jobs besides tailoring, such as gold mining, outfitting miners, and working in a brewery. He had succeeded at nothing.

Then one day, a woman came into his shop in Reno, Nevada, to order a pair of work pants for her husband. She wanted them to be sturdy, she warned, and to wear well. Most of her husband's

Jacob Davis, the inventor of riveted pants.

pants came apart, complained the woman, especially at the pockets. She paid Jacob three dollars in advance and left her order.

Davis chose the heaviest twill for these pants, cut out the fabric, and began to sew at his workbench. Suddenly he noticed the rivets that he used for horse blankets, and had an idea. If he attached the pockets to the pants with these rivets, the pockets would be stronger than just a needle and thread could make them. He made the pants that way.

The woman soon came back, took her pants, and left. The pants must have made an impression on her husband and his friends, because Davis soon had more orders than he could handle. At the end of eighteen months, he had sold 200 pairs of his riveted pants. They were made from sturdy white "duck cloth" or blue denim, both ordered from Levi Strauss, his only supplier.

After so many failures, Jacob did not want to lose this chance for success. He knew he should patent his idea before someone else discovered and made use of it. Yet, filing for a patent required money.

Before this time, Davis had filed patents for other inventions, and had never made any money on them. Would this patent be different? Jacob Davis thought it would, but Annie, his wife, disagreed. She told him not to waste any more money on worthless patents!

Jacob decided to ask for help in filing the patent. On July 2, 1872, Jacob Davis wrote a letter to Levi Strauss & Co. which would change his life as well as Levi's. The letter said he was sending by express mail two pairs of overalls, one made of blue denim and one made from ten-ounce duck. Davis went on to explain:

> The secratt of them Pents is the Rivits that I put
> in those Pockets and I found the demand so large that
> I cannot make them up fast enough. I charge for the
> Duck $3.00 and the Blue $2.50 a pear. My nabors are
> getting yealouse of these success and unless I secure it
> by Patent Papers it will soon become a general thing.
> Everybody will make them up and thare will be no
> money in it.
> Therefore Gentleman, I wish to make you a Prop-
> osition that you should take out the Latters Patent in
> my name as I am the inventor of it, the expense of it
> will be about $68, all complit....The investment for
> you is but a trifle compaired with the improvement in
> all Coarse Clothing. I use it in all Blankit Clothing
> such as Coats, Vests and Pents, and you will find it a
> very salable article at a much advenst rate....

Although Jacob Davis could not write English
well, Levi understood his meaning. He, too, had
not been educated in America, and did not allow a
few misspelled words to affect his decision. For
Levi, Jacob's letter meant a chance to expand. He
quickly agreed to pay the sixty-eight dollars required to file the patent.

The patent itself, however, was not so simple to
obtain. Each time a description of Davis's invention
was presented to the patent office, it was rejected.
Patent officials said that rivets had been used previ-
ously on a certain type of pockets in Civil War
uniforms. As a result, they could not be patented.

UNITED STATES PATENT OFFICE.

JACOB W. DAVIS, OF RENO, NEVADA, ASSIGNOR TO HIMSELF AND LEVI STRAUSS & COMPANY, OF SAN FRANCISCO, CALIFORNIA.

IMPROVEMENT IN FASTENING POCKET-OPENINGS.

Specification forming part of Letters Patent No. **139,121**, dated May 20, 1873; application filed August 9, 1872.

To all whom it may concern:

Be it known that I, JACOB W. DAVIS, of Reno, county of Washoe and State of Nevada, have invented an Improvement in Fastening Seams; and I do hereby declare the following description and accompanying drawing are sufficient to enable any person skilled in the art or science to which it most nearly appertains to make and use my said invention or improvement without further invention or experiment.

My invention relates to a fastening for pocket-openings, whereby the sewed seams are prevented from ripping or starting from frequent pressure or strain thereon; and it consists in the employment of a metal rivet or eyelet at each edge of the pocket-opening, to prevent the ripping of the seam at those points. The rivet or eyelet is so fastened in the seam as to bind the two parts of cloth which the seam unites together, so that it shall prevent the strain or pressure from coming upon the thread with which the seam is sewed.

In order to more fully illustrate and explain my invention, reference is had to the accompanying drawing, in which my invention is represented as applied to the pockets of a pair of pants.

Figure 1 is a view of my invention as applied to pants.

A is the side seam in a pair of pants, drawers, or other article of wearing apparel, which terminates at the pockets; and *b b* represent the rivets at each edge of the pocket opening. The seams are usually ripped or started by the placing of the hands in the pockets and the consequent pressure or strain upon them. To strengthen this part I employ a rivet, eyelet, or other equivalent metal stud, *b*, which I pass through a hole at the end of the seam, so as to bind the two parts of cloth together, and then head it down upon both sides so as to firmly unite the two parts. When rivets which already have one head are used, it is only necessary to head the opposite end, and a washer can be interposed, if desired, in the usual way. By this means I avoid a large amount of trouble in mending portions of seams which are subjected to constant strain.

I am aware that rivets have been used for securing seams in shoes, as shown in the patents to Geo. Houghton, No. 64,015, April 23, 1867, and to L. K. Washburn, No. 123,313, January 30, 1872; and hence I do not claim, broadly, fastening of seams by means of rivets.

Having thus described my invention, what I claim as new, and desire to secure by Letters Patent, is—

As a new article of manufacture, a pair of pantaloons having the pocket-openings secured at each edge by means of rivets, substantially in the manner described and shown, whereby the seams at the points named are prevented from ripping, as set forth.

In witness whereof I hereunto set my hand and seal.

JACOB W. DAVIS. [L. S.]

Witnesses:
JAMES C. HAGERMAN,
W. BERGMAN.

This sketch and letter describing Jacob Davis's riveted pants were accepted by the U.S. patent office.

The inventor had to explain exactly how he used the rivets and prove that he had a new idea that no one else was using.

At last, after ten months of trying, the patent was accepted. "My invention relates to a fastening for pocket-openings, whereby the sewed seams are prevented from ripping or starting from frequent pressure or strain," wrote Davis in the accepted patent application.

The idea seemed very simple, but it began a revolution in work clothes. The patent that Jacob Davis and Levi Strauss filed at that time has been illegally imitated more often than any other patent in the United States. To help make the new style of pants, Jacob Davis moved with his wife and family to San Francisco. He became the head tailor and foreman in Levi Strauss & Co.'s new factory, which made riveted clothing for the working man.

By June 2, 1873, just a few weeks after the patent was approved, Levi Strauss sold the first pair of pants with riveted pockets. One year later, Levi Strauss & Co. had distributed 21,600 pants and coats, all made from denim or heavy "duck" with riveted pockets. Miners, cowboys, lumberjacks, and other workers throughout the West eagerly bought Levi Strauss's denim clothing.

Work clothes represented only a part of Levi's business. He continued to carry a full line of dry goods and clothing from the East Coast and from overseas. But Jacob Davis's idea changed Levi's business and Levi's life. It increased his riches a great deal, it affected the style of clothing for generations to come, and it turned him and his company into a major employer.

Before 1873, Levi Strauss & Co. had paid tailors to make heavy work pants for them. These

Workers at the Levi Strauss & Co. factory in the late 1800s.

were made by individual workers in their homes, either in California or in New York. The workers were paid by the piece, according to how many pairs of pants they made.

Now, Levi had to set up a whole factory. Cutters and sewers and supervisors had to be paid. They needed sewing machines, rivets, fabric, and tools for cutting and stitching. Finally, factory laborers had to be hired.

In the 1850s, California had a great shortage of working people, and newcomers were welcomed to the state. As the population grew, though, the need for workers decreased. By the mid-1870s, there was a serious shortage of jobs. Many people believed the high level of unemployment was caused by Chinese laborers.

The Chinese had been coming to California since the gold rush. Many of them accepted very low-paying jobs that Americans did not want. They helped build America's railroads, but now the railroads were completed, and the Chinese remained in the country.

The neighborhood in San Francisco where the Chinese lived, known as Chinatown, was one of the largest Chinese communities outside the Orient. Its streets were filled with stores selling Chinese food and clothing, and its restaurants served food people were used to eating in their native land. Its residents could read the news in the many Chinese language newspapers and check for local theater performances. By the early 1870s, 2,000 Chinese laundries were operating in the city, and Chinese residents were paying one-fourth of the state's taxes.

For the average Chinese immigrant to California, work was hard and wages were very low. Most of the housing in Chinatown was crowded and unhealthy. There was a great deal of crime in the area. Many Californians were suspicious and resentful of the Chinese who lived and worked among them.

However, their presence in America had been accepted by the Burlingame Treaty, an agreement between China and the United States. Laws passed to discourage Chinese immigration and unfair treatment by white Americans did not discourage them. Like everyone else, they wanted to find work and improve their living standard.

Many American businesses took advantage of the Chinese immigrants' eagerness to work. They were hired for much lower wages than an American laborer could accept. The Chinese were satisfied, and the employers made money, but more and more American workers could not find jobs.

When Isaac Mayer Wise, a noted rabbi from the East, visited Levi's temple in 1877, he noted in his diary: "There are in this city, they say, ten thousand white men without employment....It is the Chinaman who does the factory work, the house work, the farm work, the railroad work, all sorts and kinds of manual work. But it is equally true that this cheap labor builds up California, and San Francisco especially."

By the 1870s, when unemployment reached its peak, anger against the Chinese spilled over into the streets. White workers in the Workingman's Party blamed the Chinese for their joblessness. Bitter and resentful, they formed an angry mob that surged through Chinatown. Stores were looted and burned. Some people were killed.

When Levi Strauss set up his factory, many of San Francisco's citizens, both workers and employers, were thinking and worrying about these problems. The concern about jobs and Chinese labor partly explains an advertisement displayed by the company, which proclaimed: "Our riveted goods... are made up in our Factory, under our direct supervision, and by WHITE LABOR only..."

"White labor" continued to be a trademark of Levi Strauss & Co. throughout the 1800s. Only one Chinese worked at Levi's factory at that time: the cutter. His job was to cut through layers and layers of tough denim and duck material with a long, sharp knife. Many white men had tried this work, but because it was so difficult, they were unable to do the job.

The Chinese cutter stayed on, and worked side by side with sixty white women in the factory on Fremont Street. The women sat in rows at long tables, each in front of a sewing machine. Under modern assembly-line methods, each worker is responsible for only one part of the process of making a garment. These women sewed up and finished entire garments, one at a time. First, they stitched the cut pieces of the jackets and trousers together, and then made the buttonholes and sewed on rivets. They received about three dollars per day for this work. At other factories where Chinese workers were hired, wages were much lower.

Both Levi and Jacob Davis believed the guarantee of "white labor only" was a way to help their country. The company tried to offer a well-made product without taking advantage of immigrant labor.

Levi's riveted clothing appealed to many people. Although other manufacturers often sold a similar product for less money, the waist-high overalls made from Double X denim, and reinforced with copper rivets, continued to lead the market. After overcoming all challenges to Jacob Davis's patent, the company could claim that it was the "sole proprietor and manufacturer of the celebrated, patented, riveted duck and denim clothing."

So that the buyers could recognize its brand, the company added a special kind of stitching to the pockets, shaped in a crossed, double V. This special trademark was sewn in orange thread to match the copper color of the rivets. It can still be seen on Levi's jeans today.

An early advertisement for Levi Strauss & Co.'s copper-riveted overalls.

Levi Strauss's pants and jackets were sold mostly in California. But the company also had sales representatives throughout the western United States and Canada, as well as in Mexico, the Hawaiian Islands, Tahiti, and New Zealand.

Levi himself continued to prosper along with his company. Still unmarried, he was growing stout on a combination of his sister Fanny's cooking and elegant dinner parties. Through his family business and real estate interests, he was also growing richer.

Since he had come to California, much had changed for Levi. Most of the changes had been good, but he could recall sad times as well.

Chapter/Six

Call me Levi

One of Levi's saddest memories was of David Stern's death on January 2, 1874. David, only fifty-one when he died, had been Levi's friend and partner for many years. A devoted husband and father to eight sons and daughters, he was an important member of San Francisco's Jewish community. Levi and David had shared twenty-one years as business associates. Together they had planned and built a company of which they were proud. The newspapers called Stern "the highly respected pioneer merchant."

At the funeral the next day, Levi and the family rode to the cemetery in several black-draped coaches. The coachmen dressed in black for the occasion, and the windows were curtained off from the curious stares of the public. Many friends and business associates followed the family coaches to the burial ground and listened to Rabbi Cohn recite the traditional graveside prayer for the dead: "Magnified and sanctified is the name of the Living God...." and ending with a prayer for peace.

After the funeral service, Levi returned with the family to the house on Powell Street. Following Jewish custom, they remained at home for several days, receiving callers who came to comfort them. During the first week, the house was filled with people. Then Levi and the family went back to work.

Levi Strauss & Co. was now a large enterprise which employed several hundred workers. However, without David Stern, some changes had to be made.

The company had never been without a member of the Stern family. Now that Fanny was a widow, she wanted the Stern sons to share in their father's legacy. Having no children of his own, Levi had accepted Fanny and David's sons as his heirs long before. But when David died, his children were barely full grown. Twenty-three-year-old Jacob, now the oldest, was working as a store clerk on Montgomery Street. Sigmund, next in line, was just seventeen, and Louis and Abraham were even younger.

Jacob agreed to leave his clerking job and come to work for Levi in the Battery Street building. A sober young man, Jacob soon earned a place for himself in the company. His cousins, Moses and Henry Sahlein, worked there as well. Another generation of Sterns and Sahleins were getting ready to manage the family business.

Later that year, the Strausses, the Sterns, and the Sahleins attended a very special event. Levi's sister Mary and her husband, William Sahlein, had come out to San Francisco years ago to join in partnership with Levi and David. When Mary died, William was left to raise their three children alone.

After David Stern's death, William Sahlein, still a widower, spent many hours together with Fanny. William was lonely without a wife, and Fanny wanted a husband. They decided to get married.

Once the rabbi performed the marriage, there was much work to be done. The Powell Street house, as large as it was, would be too small for the combined families. There were thirteen people in all: Fanny's seven children and William's three; the new couple, Fanny and William; and Levi Strauss, an important and honored member of the household. The house also had to be large enough for guests such as Levi's brother Louis and his nephew Nathan, who spent many months a year in San Francisco.

With much excitement Levi and the family pre-pared to move. The new house, located at 621 Leav-enworth Street, was larger than either of their previ-ous homes had been. Although it was not as elegant and luxurious as some of the mansions in the neigh-borhood, it was a home that suited them well.

Typical of San Francisco houses built during this period, it had a columned entrance, a center hall, and a formal parlor. Beautiful carpets covered the polished floors, and the walls were hung with paintings. Upstairs were the family bedrooms, and beyond them the servants' quarters. In most of the fashionable homes in San Francisco, a large bay window let in the sunlight.

Levi quickly settled into the comfortable, spa-cious mansion. His routines did not change; he simply walked to work by a longer and slightly different route. Levi believed that walking and fresh air were good for the health.

Like most of the German-Jewish businessmen of the neighborhood, Levi left the house at 9:00 A.M. and made his way toward the business district. The prosperous merchants whom Levi met along the way all lived and worked nearby. Their wives visited, and their children married each other. The men would nod pleasantly as they passed on the street, exchange a few words about business or the weather, and go on to their offices.

Approaching his Battery Street headquarters, Levi Strauss would stop to greet his neighbors. The first shop on the block belonged to Leo Metzger, who sold wine and brandies. Next to him were William Fleisher, a manufacturer of hats and caps, and Blumenthal and Company, glove manufacturers.

Once inside his own columned doorway, Levi greeted his employees before settling into his office at the back of the four-story building. The head cashier, Philip Fisher, and Albert Hirschfeld, a loyal worker, waited for Levi's pleasant "good morning" each day at 10:00 A.M.

After quickly examining the previous day's sales, Levi went out onto the floor. Here, he could watch the company's daily activities, and chat with longtime customers who came to purchase his goods for their own shops. He urged the clerks to call him "Levi" instead of the more formal "Mr. Strauss," and always had a smile and an encouraging word for a young worker. If he saw that a junior clerk was working hard and doing a good job, he would make sure the clerk received a promotion.

In this way, Levi Strauss kept up with his workers and his business. A few blocks away, Jacob

Levi Strauss & Co. workers in front of the Battery Street headquarters.

Davis directed the work at the new factory, produc-ing "overalls" as fast as possible. Levi often went there also to make sure the work was going as planned. With his black frock coat and top hat, he was a familiar sight looking into the door of the factory, greeting the workers and talking with Jacob.

After lunch, Levi usually spent the rest of his working day at stockholders' meetings, conferences with real estate brokers, and board meetings. Then

Levi returned to the Battery Street building, where he and Philip Fisher, his bookkeeper and friend, went over the books and wrote business letters.

It was a full day, which ended late. Yet it was not all work for Levi. He enjoyed dining and often gave dinner parties for his friends.

The Saint Francis Hotel was a favorite place for Levi's private gatherings. Here, in elegant private dining rooms, Levi met with and entertained friends. Sometimes he invited his nephew Nathan Strauss from New York, and Sigmund Stern, Fanny's son, to join him at the hotel for parties. Sigmund enjoyed the social scene with Uncle Levi, and sometimes brought along his own friends.

In spite of the parties and good times, neither Levi nor any of his nephews ever got involved in scandals. It was easy to get into trouble in San Francisco, which boasted "naughty rooms" above the fashionable cafés, and where hard drinking was a tradition. Although Levi's nephew Nathan was known as a young man who liked to have a good time with the ladies, he never disgraced his family or got into any trouble.

Levi Strauss, who was among the city's richest citizens, was known as a man of fairness and honesty. However, a person who was so well known and wealthy had to expect some complaints.

"Tightfisted," was the way columnist Isadore Choynski described Levi Strauss in the Jewish publication, the *American Israelite*. He blamed Levi, along with all the rich Jews of San Francisco, for ignoring or neglecting many worthy projects. After failing to raise fifty dollars each for charity from several of the city's Jewish millionaires, Choynski said: "These fellows are more likely to plunk down twice as much on a pair of aces."

The *San Francisco Post* was also critical of the actions of wealthy city residents such as Levi Strauss. Levi, Leland Stanford, the railroad magnate, and millionaire businessman Isaac Friedlander had signed a memorial thanking James Lick for donating an observatory to the University of California. "If these gentlemen have such a profound appreciation for Mr. Lick's action," said an editorial, "why don't they show it by going and doing likewise?" And in the meantime, suggested the same writer, the community might appreciate them more "if they were to make a point of paying something like a fair share of the taxes." This last line was a reminder that many of San Francisco's poorer citizens had no work and not enough to eat, while the city's rich businesspeople enjoyed every luxury and sometimes tried to avoid taxes.

The tax collector came regularly to residential

streets where the rich merchants lived. He estimated the worth of each family's possessions and
charged the tax accordingly. The city's top families joked that when they saw the tax collector in
the neighborhood, the ladies would rush to hide
their furs, jewels, and expensive china.

The charges made against Levi Strauss were not
well founded. Although not yet among the largest
contributors to charity, Levi Strauss had already
earned a reputation for "liberality" (generosity) in
matters of money. He paid his taxes and contributed
regularly to Temple Emanu-el, the Eureka Benevolent Society, and other worthy causes.

Levi could hardly ignore his responsibilities
to the community. On July 24, 1877, his name
appeared on a list of San Francisco's citizens who
had $4 million or more. Levi made an effort to use
some of that wealth in ways that would benefit his
community and state.

Chapter/Seven

My life is my business

At fifty-six, Levi Strauss was busy, well fed, and more successful than ever. His top hat now covered his thinning hair and shiny, high forehead. His face was smooth and clean shaven except for a goatee, a small beard, covering his chin. People said he looked distinguished.

As Levi had grown older, the city he lived in had changed almost completely. The rough mining town, with wooden planking for streets, now had neat brick sidewalks. Wagons and fancy carriages filled the roadways. Where once there had been tents and makeshift stores built on pilings, now there were fine shops and elegant hotels. Beautiful homes had spread well beyond the waterfront up into the hills.

As an older man, Levi Strauss had thinning hair and a goatee.

The city, and Levi with it, had survived two major earthquakes and numerous fires. Linked to the East by telegraph and rail, and with a port that welcomed ships from all over the world, San Francisco in 1885 looked ahead to a glorious future.

Even more than the city he lived in, the people in Levi's life had changed. David Stern, and later his brother Louis Strauss in New York and his brother-in-law William Sahlein, had died. His nephews filled those empty places in the company, but not in his heart.

Now Fanny was gone, too. Of the original family, only Levi and Jonas remained, and Jonas was far away in New York.

Yet for Levi, getting older was not always sad. He had enjoyed watching his nieces and nephews grow up, marry, and have families of their own. First Jacob, the oldest, announced his marriage to his cousin Rosa Sahlein. This was followed by the engagements and marriages of his nieces Caroline and Hattie Stern, and then the Sahlein nephews.

Levi was one of the few who had not married.

"I am a bachelor," he would later tell a reporter, "and I fancy on that account I need to work more, for my entire life is my business."

Beyond the factory and the "store," as he called the company, his business now included growing real estate holdings. In fact, Levi owned a large part of downtown San Francisco.

Major companies wanted Levi to serve as a director. The board of directors was made up of prominent people who examined the business, and advised the management on how to make the most profits. Levi Strauss served as a director of the Spring Valley Water Company, the San Fernando Land and Milling Company, the San Francisco Gas Company, and the London, Liverpool, and Globe Insurance Company.

In addition to real estate and company boards, Levi Strauss worked to strengthen his own company. In 1875, with two friends, he purchased the Mission and Pacific Woolen Mills. The Levi Strauss & Co. factory used blankets to line some of their work clothes. These riveted ''blanket clothes,'' as Jacob Davis had called them in his first letter to Levi, had become a highly successful item. The purchase of the woolen mills meant the company could buy the blankets it needed for much less money, and increase its profit on the clothes in which they were used.

With all these outside interests, Levi spent less time with his original company. However, he never stayed away from the family business for very long. Although his nephews ran the office, and

Jacob Davis supervised the factory, he was still needed for major decisions.

Since David Stern's death in 1874, his oldest son, Jacob, had become an important company manager. Then Louis started as a cashier under Philip Fisher's supervision. Several years later, Sigmund, the fun-loving bachelor with a head for business—the one who was most like his uncle Levi—also joined the company. He began work as a buyer.

Under Jacob Davis's watchful eye, the factory had expanded its operations. In addition to the "waist-high overalls," it had begun to produce a successful new line of work shirts.

Levi Strauss & Co. work clothes were becoming well known outside California, too. In spite of the high cost of shipping by rail, and the increasing competition from other firms, there was a growing demand for Levi's high-quality products. Cowboys in Texas, lumberjacks in Washington, and miners in Canada bought his clothing.

Even in Paris, France, people knew of Levi's overalls and blanket clothing. In 1878 he had helped organize an exhibit of California products in France, and his work clothes were part of the display.

During the 1880s, Levi Strauss & Co. introduced its new label. Made of leather, it was

Western miners around 1870 wearing Levi Strauss & Co. work pants.

attached to the back of the waistband in the same place as the old oilcloth label. The new label also had the same picture: two horses trying to pull apart a pair of Double X Denim pants. To the firm's customers, waist-high denim overalls were known as the "Two Horse Brand." The Levi Strauss & Co. guarantee promised "a new pair free" if their pants ripped. They rarely did.

Levi's pants lasted so well because of their pat-

The company's label advertised its riveted work pants as the "Two Horse Brand."

ented riveted construction. But in a few years that patent would expire, and then anyone could make riveted pants exactly the way the Strauss firm did. Although the company still sold other items such as its imported goods, women's clothes, underwear, and pajamas, the work clothes had become the most important part of the firm's business. Levi had to prepare for the time when his company would not be the only maker of these pants.

Levi didn't want to lose that market to other manufacturers who could make clothing for less because they used cheaper labor. Still, he had promised to employ "whites only" to operate his machines and produce his clothing, even though they were paid twice as much as Chinese laborers. Levi sold his work clothes mainly to American working people who needed the jobs to support their families. Without work, he thought, they would not have money to buy his clothes.

Ever since the mob of angry white workers had raged through Chinatown, Levi had believed his policy was right. The 250 sewing machine operators in his factory were all white women, except for the Chinese cutter. In the headquarters on Battery Street, white men were employed. Levi hired a Chinese worker only when he could not fill a job in any other way.

By today's standards and values, Levi Strauss's ideas about hiring workers appear to be wrong. But in his time people saw things differently. Levi was respected for his commitment to American labor. His customers understood that he could have made more money by running his factory the way others did.

In 1890, when the patent expired, Levi was ready for competition from other firms. His company kept its high-quality work pants, referred to in the catalog as number 501. Those would not change. In addition, Levi Strauss & Co. would make its own cheaper version of the denim waist-high overalls to compete with those made by other firms.

Besides competition from other producers of work clothes, a serious threat to Levi's business came from owners of railroads. During the 1860s, the Union Pacific Railroad had built westward from Omaha, while the Central Pacific moved eastward, laying track to complete the final link of the transcontinental railroad. When the last spike was driven in 1869, people believed that all the transportation difficulties of the West were over. But now there were new problems.

Price fixing by California's railroad owners led to freight rates that were much too high. A merchant in northern California could order clothing shipped from Chicago for less money than it cost to send the same order from San Francisco! Prices for shipping goods theatened not only Levi Strauss & Co., but also many other San Francisco businesses. Without them, the city could not continue to grow. But if an alternate route from the East to the West could be developed, it would give the railroads competition and force their rates down.

In 1891, Levi joined thirty-nine other San Francisco businessmen who had been hurt by the policy of the railroads. Each of the men pledged $1,000 from his own funds to find the best route for a new railroad between San Francisco and Salt Lake City, Utah. After the survey was completed, the men planned to raise the rest of the money by selling shares of stock to other businesspeople.

Despite their enthusiasm, the plan failed, and Levi Strauss looked for other solutions. He firmly believed that his efforts would save his business and ensure the future growth of San Francisco. Levi had already learned that the Los Angeles Chamber of Commerce was trying to build a railroad to the north. If it succeeded, he believed, Los Angeles would overtake San Francisco as the leading city in the state.

Once more, money was needed, and again Levi gave his share. This time he contributed $25,000 toward a new rail line that his friend Claus Spreckels hoped to develop.

An important supporter for this new plan was William Randolph Hearst, a young journalist and owner of the San Francisco *Examiner*. Hearst, a friend of Sigmund Stern, had attended Levi Strauss's dinner parties and knew him well. When he published articles about the new railroad in his paper, it became an accepted idea. Money was raised from the city's leading citizens, and work began on the San Francisco and San Joaquin Valley Railroad.

Unfortunately, Levi's investment in this project ended in another disappointment. Spreckels, who owned most of the railroad's stock, sold his interests to another railroad company without asking permission from his associates. The new management soon joined other railroads in charging high shipping rates and ended any chance for lowering prices. With his hopes shattered, Levi Strauss left the railroad business.

During those years of involvement with the railroads, Levi Strauss had not neglected his own company. By 1890 it was incorporated. That meant it was legally divided into shares. Levi owned 55 percent of the shares, and the rest was divided equally among the seven Stern brothers and sisters.

At this time, Jacob Stern ran the offices and supervised the sales at the Battery Street building. Sigmund Stern was the company's buyer, and Louis helped with the finances. Abraham was still too young to work for the company.

In 1890 Levi was sixty-one years old, and he had given up most of his parties. Occasionally, he entertained friends or dined with Sigmund and Louis, who were still bachelors like Levi. Two years later, that situation would change, too.

Sigmund, on a trip to Europe with Louis, met Rosalie Meyer and fell in love. Rosalie was twenty-

Sigmund Stern, Levi Strauss's favorite nephew and the company's buyer.

three years old and the daughter of a prominent California Jewish banker, Eugene Meyer.

Sigmund sent Uncle Levi a telegram asking his permission to propose marriage to Rosalie. Next he wired his brother Jacob: "Am well, happy, contented and engaged. Could I be more?"

After the excitement of the wedding and the party that followed, Levi continued his usual daily routine. He still lived on Leavenworth Street, now with Jacob and Rosa and their children. He left his house at nine, was in the office at ten, went to meetings, and took care of business.

In a rare interview given in 1895, Levi hinted at the loneliness he sometimes felt.

"I don't think money brings friends to its owner," he said. "In fact, the result is quite the contrary." In the same article, he maintained that large fortunes "do not cause happiness to their owners." He went on to explain: "Immediately those who possess them become slaves to their wealth. They must devote their lives to caring for their possessions."

As Levi grew older, he looked for ways to use his money to help others. For many years, he had donated money to the Pacific Hebrew Orphan Asylum and the Eureka Benevolent Society. In 1897, Levi's friend Jacob Reinstein suggested that he contribute to a scholarship fund for the University of California. Levi agreed, and wrote a letter to the state board of regents. If the California legislature would create twenty-eight scholarships, wrote Levi, he would match them with twenty-eight scholarships of his own. The board of regents accepted his offer.

As the nineteenth century drew to a close, Levi looked back at the seventy-one years of his

life. He had traveled halfway around the world—
from Buttenheim, Bavaria, across the ocean to
New York, to Kentucky, and around the Horn to
San Francisco. Beginning as an inexperienced immigrant, he had become a successful merchant and a
respected millionaire. He had watched his adopted
country grow from a small, undeveloped group of
states into a great nation. In his lifetime, gold had
been discovered, a civil war had been fought, railroads built, and fortunes made and lost. There had
been sad times and happy times; successes and dis-
appointments. Levi could hardly believe that so
much time had passed.

As New Year's Eve, December 31, 1899, arrived, Levi and his family waited for the stroke of
midnight. His nieces and nephews awakened their
young children to greet the new century, and
talked about what the future held for them.

As for Levi, his brothers and sisters were gone.
With a lifetime of experience already behind him,
he wondered how much of the new century he
would be privileged to share.

Chapter/Eight

A man with a grand character

With the new century came new challenges. Levi Strauss & Co. was still growing, but Levi was less and less involved in the business that bore his name. Although he still came to his office on Battery Street, Jacob and Sigmund Stern handled most of the daily affairs of the company.

In his seventies, Levi's biggest challenges were keeping fit and watching his health. His doctors—all three of them—said Levi Strauss had a problem with his heart. Each doctor examined him carefully and told him he needed to rest more.

His family and friends worried, but complete retirement, they knew, was not possible for him. "A man who once forms the habit of being busy," Levi had said, cannot retire and be contented. Unlike other men who gave up work, Levi Strauss would not be "wearing himself out" trying to rest.

When Jacob Stern hired a nurse for his aging uncle, Levi let him have his way. The nurse would make his nephews and nieces happy, and would not change anything for him. Levi still found the time for work, but his nurse was a well-trained man who kept him from doing too much.

Giving money to charity continued to occupy his time, too. The Levi Strauss university scholarships, which he established in 1897, provided enough money to pay for twenty-eight college students each year.

Through a lifetime of hard work, Levi Strauss had made a fortune. Once he had said, "my entire life is my business." Now in his old age, that was no longer true. He looked for other ways to leave a mark on the world.

Although Levi had no wife and children of his own, he was a true "family man." With increasing pleasure, he watched a growing group of grand-nieces and nephews. First there had been only Jacob and Rosa's children. Now Levi had several more—Sigmund and Rosalie's little girl, the Sahlein youngsters, and the children of Fanny's daughters, Caroline and Hattie. The Strauss clan was expanding at a fast rate.

These children were the new generation in the West. In the East, where his brothers had made their homes, there was also a new generation.

Levi Strauss had outlived even some of his nephews and nieces. As he entered his seventy-third year, he felt more tired than usual. When his family and the doctors recommended a vacation, Levi took their advice and went to the Hotel Del Monte, a fashionable resort north of San Francisco.

The Del Monte attracted only the richest Americans. The elite of California were there, and Levi Strauss, well known and well liked, was counted among them. People he hardly knew asked his advice and wanted the secrets of his success. Levi enjoyed helping others, and always tried to answer.

Pleasant surroundings, people who tried to please him, good food, and a kindly nurse to make sure he was comfortable—all helped to make the vacation a success. Levi returned home feeling much better.

At Levi Strauss & Co., there was still work to do. On Monday morning, September 22, 1902, Levi walked from his home on Leavenworth Street to the Battery Street offices. He walked slowly, as the doctors had advised, and enjoyed the fine weather of early fall. Once in his office, Levi reviewed the sales figures and chatted with the workers. Everyone remarked at how fit he looked after his holiday.

By Tuesday, however, Levi realized that he was still a sick man. He awoke feeling tired and ill, and stayed at home. "Not serious," the doctors declared, just a slight "congestion of the liver." They prescribed some medicine for Levi and assured him that he would be feeling better soon.

By Friday morning, Levi's condition showed some improvement. That evening he felt well enough to eat dinner with the family. He joked with the children and acted as lighthearted as he used to before his heart condition began troubling him.

After dinner, Levi's nurse helped him settle into bed, and remained awake to watch. Shortly before midnight, the nurse heard a moan. He rushed over, leaned across the bed, and asked: "How are you feeling?"

"Oh, about as comfortable as I can under the circumstances," answered Levi in a soft voice.

Levi Strauss turned his head on his pillow, closed his eyes, and went to sleep. The nurse, sensing something was wrong, hurried to call the family. By the time they arrived at his bedside, Levi Strauss was dead.

The funeral was held in the Strauss home, on Sunday, September 28, 1902. The San Francisco

The scenes shown on this medal honor the achievements of Levi Strauss.

Evening Post reported that "men from every station in life were present to pay their tribute of respect to the memory of the dead millionaire." His richest friends and business associates, and the machine operators at his factory, crowded into the house on Leavenworth Street. They strained to hear the words of Rabbi Voorsanger of Temple Emanu-el.

After reciting several psalms, the rabbi spoke of Levi Strauss with great admiration and respect.

He talked about his good deeds more than his success in business, reminding the crowd that "Levi Strauss was a man...with a grand character, who loved peace and pursued it, whose word was his bond and his promise and obligation."

At the end of the speech, the body of Levi Strauss was carried out past his family, business associates, and 200 employees of Levi Strauss & Co. Each of them felt that Levi had been a friend.

In San Francisco's business district, flags flew at half mast all day, and businesses were closed. In a special meeting, the board of trade passed a resolution praising Levi Strauss as a man "in the front ranks of San Francisco's commercial activities." They called him a "liberal, public-spirited citizen," whose love of humanity went beyond race, religion, or creed.

A few weeks later, Levi's nephews and nieces assembled to hear the will that Levi Strauss had written just one week before his death. There were no surprises for anyone. Jacob, Sigmund, Louis, and Abraham Stern knew that they were to inherit the business. They had already been running Levi Strauss & Co. for many years, with their uncle's agreement.

True to his character as a family man, Levi remembered all his relatives. His nephews and nieces and their children each received a bequest of money from his estate.

Two of Levi's longtime employees also received gifts. Finally, he left large amounts of money to the charities of many different faiths for which he had worked during his lifetime.

Levi Strauss's estate was worth $6 million. And yet, Levi had given his family far more than money. He had left a legacy of hard work, honesty, fair play, and helpfulness that would set an example for generations to come.

Chapter/Nine

Levi Strauss & Co.— after Levi

The Levi Strauss story does not end with Levi's death. The company's growth in the years that followed is just as remarkable as the life of its founder.

Levi's firm continued with Jacob Stern at its head. Sigmund and Abraham worked with him, while Louis lived in New York and ran the eastern branch of the business.

Suddenly on April 18, 1906, another earthquake—the worst in the history of San Francisco—shook the city. Rabbi Voorsanger of Temple Emanu-el, commenting on this natural disaster, said: "The abyss yawned at our feet and it seemed that with the overturning of the world we would be lost forever."

The enormous destructive power of the 1906 San Francisco earthquake left much of the city in ruins.

Within a few minutes, the life of the Stern family was turned upside down. The building on Battery Street, home to Levi Strauss & Co. for so many years, burned almost completely. The company's Donahue Street factory was seriously damaged.

Jacob Stern was on a European vacation at the time. Sigmund and Rosalie, Abraham and his wife Elise, and all their children fled their shaky homes. They camped together in Sigmund's back yard while the aftershocks and fires continued throughout the city.

After the earthquake, the two Stern brothers managed the business from Abraham's house. They used part of a temporary factory in Oakland as their showroom, and began building a new factory. Their rebuilt headquarters moved a few doors down to 98 Battery Street. This corner would remain the company's home until 1973.

Through all the problems caused by the earthquake, Levi Strauss & Co. continued to pay wages to 350 employees even though they could not work. Most firms in San Francisco did not do this. The company extended credit, with little or no interest, to the merchants who bought its products. This helped people whose shops were destroyed by the earthquake.

Because of the commitment of its owners, Levi Strauss & Co. came back stronger than ever. The following year, in the bank panic of 1907, the company relied on money from the four Stern brothers to stay in business. Using their own funds to cover expenses, the partners offered credit to their customers while the banks refused loans.

Jacob Stern, as the oldest heir, followed his Uncle Levi as member and director of many different boards. He gave money to make the twenty-eight Levi Strauss scholarships a permanent award by the University of California. Jacob and Rosa, and Sigmund and Rosalie Stern were millionaires now. They became art collectors and music patrons. Sadly, Abraham, the youngest brother, died of food poisoning in 1912.

Jacob Davis, the tailor who had invented riveted clothing and led Levi into large-scale manufacturing, had retired. Many of the business decisions were now made by his twenty-nine-year-old son, Simon, who managed the new factory.

In 1919, after forty-five years with Levi Strauss & Co., Jacob Stern also prepared to retire. Sigmund needed help if the business was to continue. He asked his daughter Elise's husband, Walter Haas, to join the company. Haas, thirty years old and just out of the army, had worked briefly in his family's very successful grocery business.

Walter Haas realized that Levi Strauss & Co. was a firm with large national sales, but a relatively small profit. Because it did not fire its older employees, and continued to pay the salaries of retired workers, it had higher expenses and smaller profits than other companies.

Walter Haas looked for ways to make the company grow. One of the ways he tried to do this was to eliminate the Koverall line of children's play clothes. Though this product was a success on the market, it was too expensive to make. Simon Davis, the man who had developed the Koverall line, threatened to leave.

With these problems, plus the knowledge that Sigmund Stern would soon retire, Walter Haas turned to his cousin and brother-in-law, Daniel Koshland, to join him in the family business. In a final clash over the Koverall line, Simon Davis left Levi Strauss & Co. to start his own business. Walter Haas and Daniel Koshland concentrated on finding ways the company could make a profit and improve their product.

"A new pair of pants free if they rip" was a Levi Strauss guarantee. If the pants ever did rip, they would be examined and the defect corrected. Like Levi Strauss, the new partners believed that "quality would tell."

By 1931, during the Great Depression, 12 million Americans were unemployed, and Levi Strauss & Co.'s sales dropped dangerously low. To keep as many people working as possible, the firm put its employees on a shorter work week. Through the 1930s, the company struggled. Then, slowly, sales rose, and workers returned to full-time employment.

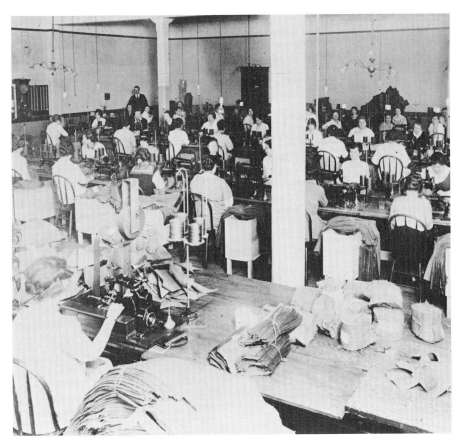

By the early 1900s, sewing machine operators at Levi Strauss & Co. used an assembly-line method of producing clothes.

At this time Levi Strauss & Co.'s main product was the 501 waist overalls. They had remained almost the same as when Jacob Davis designed and patented the first pair. But gradually, these began to change.

First, the copper rivets on the back pockets were covered so they would not scratch saddles, cars, and school seats. Then Haas decided to eliminate the single copper rivet that had been placed below the front opening of the pants. He made this decision after he stood near a campfire, and learned what the cowboys who wore them had discovered: the copper rivet heated up and burned the wearer! By 1936 a small red tag was added to the side of the back pocket. This has remained a Levi's trademark to this day.

Small changes in style continued to be made. Buttons for suspenders were replaced by belt loops. In the 1950s zipper closings replaced the buttons. Still, the famous ten-ounce denim fabric that Levi Strauss had originally sent to Jacob Davis so long ago remained the same.

About 1939, college students began to wear Levi Strauss 501 Double X denim pants. This was the beginning of a new image for work clothes. By 1942, *Levi's* was adopted as the official name for the 501s, now called *jeans*.

During World War II, Levi Strauss & Co. began to change its hiring practices. The company was among the first in the United States to hire black workers in its factories. "We Hire Freely," was the sign that was now hung in the Valencia Street factory in San Francisco. When new factories were built in the South, the management also insisted on fair hiring practices. Unlike other companies, Levi Strauss & Co. refused to keep black workers separate or hire them only for low-paying jobs.

As the company grew and changed, Walter and Elise Haas's two sons, Walter, Jr., and Peter, prepared to take over from their father. The Haas sons inherited a strong and successful company. By 1948 the Levi's trademark had become so popular that it was being used for all blue denim pants.

Levi's business had begun in 1853 as a small wholesale firm, which also made work clothes. Now the company that bore his name was a national manufacturer. In 1953, 100 years later, Daniel Koshland and Walter Haas marked the company's anniversary by establishing a foundation to contribute money to worthwhile charities and institutions in San Francisco.

In the 1950s a new American legend brought even more success for Levi Strauss & Co. It began with a movie, *Rebel Without a Cause*, starring James Dean, a handsome young actor. Young people identified with Dean and began to wear the kind of clothes he wore in the movie: Levi's, boots, and a T shirt. Although James Dean died in a car accident shortly after the release of the movie, his character became part of American culture. Marlon Brando, another young actor, followed the James Dean tradition in his movie, *The Wild Ones*. Brando rode a motorcycle and wore a leather jacket over his 501 jeans.

By the mid-1950s, Levi's and T shirts had become a favorite of the young generation. In order to keep up with the demand for jeans, 2,500 workers in factories all over the United States were kept busy sewing Levi's.

In the 1960s, America's youth began protesting against United States involvement in the Vietnam War, and rebelling against how the older generation thought and acted. Levi's jeans became their uniform. Levi's were especially popular on college campuses among anti-establishment protesters.

The 1960s was also the time of the Civil Rights movement. Because they were sensitive to the needs of American blacks, and working people in general, Levi Strauss & Co. developed a community affairs department and community involvement teams.

Since that time, a company-supported charitable foundation has been distributing money to a variety of health, cultural, and human resources projects. Fair hiring practices, profit sharing, loans for workers, and cost-of-living increases for retired employees are some other ways in which the company fulfills its corporate responsibility. More recently, affirmative action programs have helped minorities and women become plant managers, engineers, and drivers. These programs did not stop even when Levi Strauss & Co. was in trouble.

The tremendous growth in the 1960s, and the expansion of marketing and manufacturing into Europe, led to a decision in 1970 to "go public." This meant that Levi Strauss & Co. would no longer be owned by the family. There would be a public offering of stock, a board of directors, and a new way of making decisions. For the first time, the company president would not be part of the family.

"I assure you we expect to conduct our business as we have in the past," Walter Haas, Jr., said. He promised to recognize "our responsibilities to our shareholders, to our employees, to our customers, to our community, and to our nation..."

But once the company was public, the family had less control over the quality of its products and the growth of the firm. Levi Strauss & Co. overexpanded and began to lose money.

"Levi Strauss busts its britches," was the headline for a 1973 article in *Fortune* magazine, a leading business publication. The company had lost $12 million in Europe.

It took a great deal of work to recover from those losses. By 1974, though, the losses were under control, and the company had more than a billion dollars in sales.

Levi's still remained one of the most popular pieces of clothing in the country. In 1977, President

Jimmy Carter was shown wearing Levi's in the White House. In 1984, Levi Strauss & Co. was the official outfitter for the United States Olympic Team. All these developments were part of a revolution in clothing which Levi Strauss & Co. has helped to create.

The crisis of the 1970s led to an important decision: the company would return to being a family business. Robert D. Haas, new head of the firm, and his cousin Peter are the fifth generation of the Strauss and Stern family to head Levi Strauss & Co.

On August 30, 1985, the Haas cousins took a loan of $1.485 billion and purchased a majority of their own stock. Today, 99.8 percent of the company's stock belongs to family members.

The company, now in beautiful new quarters on a street named for it—Levi's Plaza—is the world's largest manufacturer of blue jeans. It employs 35,000 people and has 40,000 retail outlets in seventy countries. The business that Levi Strauss built in San Francisco has maintained a reputation for quality workmanship, concern for workers, and an interest in charitable giving that sets an example for the world.

Appendix /

The California Gold Rush

Why search for gold? Why is gold so important that hundreds of thousands of people would rush halfway across the world for a chance to find this metal?

Gold is a chemical element that people have always liked because of its color and hardness. It is easy to work with, but almost impossible to destroy. Precious objects, coins, and ornaments made from gold were valued by cultures as far apart as Egypt and Colombia. For these and other reasons, people rushed to California when gold was discovered there.

California was once Mexican territory. Although rumors of gold had persisted in the area, no discovery had been made, and the Mexican government did nothing to develop mining interests. It did encourage development and settlement by awarding grants of property to individual people.

The United States government had wanted to buy California for some time to extend the fast-growing nation to the Pacific Coast. Mexico, however, did not want to sell.

When fighting broke out between Mexican and U.S. forces, the two nations declared war. On July 9, 1846, U.S. Navy ships sailed into San Francisco Bay, and Captain John B. Montgomery raised the American flag at a place called Portsmouth Square. Less than six months later, the town was renamed San Francisco. With the discovery of gold, it was destined to become one of the major cities of the country.

The Treaty of Guadalupe Hidalgo ended the war between Mexico and its northern neighbor. In 1848, the United States officially acquired California as well as large areas of what is now the American Southwest. In exchange, the U.S. government gave the Mexican government $15 million. From then on, the future of the area was in American hands.

The story of the California gold rush goes back to John Augustus Sutter, a Swiss immigrant who came to the New World in 1834. He had fled from his native land as a result of personal debt and bankruptcy. Leaving his wife and family behind in Switzerland, he sought to build a new life.

In this new land, where no one knew about his past, John Sutter pretended to be an ex-captain of the Royal Swiss Guard of the king of France. With persuasion and charm, he convinced the Mexican government to grant him 50,000 acres in California. In return for the land, he agreed to build a fortified post on the northern border of Mexican territory, near the American River.

John Sutter created a small empire on his land. Within its boundaries lived local native Americans and an assorted group of Mexicans, Hawaiians, and Mormons. These people all worked for Sutter. They harvested his wheat fields, herded his cattle, and operated his flour mills, liquor distillery, and stores.

Sutter's empire was well established when the United States took possession of California in 1846. Before the Treaty of Guadalupe Hidalgo had confirmed American ownership, he had decided to build a sawmill there as well.

In mid-January 1848, Sutter's builder, James W. Marshall, was working on the mill. As he wrote later in his journal: "There upon the rock, about six inches beneath the surface of the water, I discovered gold...Four days afterwards, I went to the Fort for provisions and carried with me about three ounces of gold."

The shiny, brass-colored metal that Marshall had found was first brought to John Sutter and submitted to the tests of hammering and boiling in lye. If it was gold, it would not break or be corroded. When the metal passed both tests, the men were convinced that it was indeed gold.

John Sutter and James Marshall became partners, but there were many things to do before they could announce their discovery. Sutter and Marshall continued work on the sawmill, pledging the workers to silence.

Knowing that his original claim to the land came from Mexico, Sutter attempted to secure title to his property. He did this by making an agreement with the local native Americans to lease it from them. Then he sent a messenger to the new U.S. governor of California in an effort to establish clear ownership of the land under U.S. law. But Governor Mason refused to accept Sutter as the owner, insisting that the United States did not recognize the right of the native Americans to sell or lease land.

While Sutter's claim to the territory was being disputed, the two partners tried to keep their discovery to themselves. News spread, however, in spite of their attempts at secrecy. By the middle of March, the secret had leaked out.

At first, there was only a small article in the

John Sutter played a key role in the events that led to the California gold rush.

Californian, a local San Francisco paper, under the headline "Gold Mine Found." No one paid much attention to it. Sam Brannon, a Mormon leader and an ambitious businessman, noticed the article and went up to the American River to check it out.

Sam Brannon owned a store at Sutter's Fort, and he also owned his own newspaper. When he discovered that there was indeed gold on Sutter's land, he reprinted the news in his own paper. People read it in states such as Missouri and Ohio. By announcing the discovery of gold, Brannon hoped for large profits. He anticipated that the miners who came would buy supplies from his stores, read his newspaper, and make him rich.

When his article still did not attract many gold seekers, Brannon resorted to other methods. According to legend, Sam Brannon ran through the streets of San Francisco, holding high a bottle filled with gold dust and shouting "Gold! Gold! Gold from the American River!" His cry excited the citizens of San Francisco, and thousands rushed to stake claims to every foot of soil in the valley.

Neither Brannon nor Sutter and Marshall were prepared for the madness that began when people actually believed there was gold. Eager gold seekers overran Sutter's property and the surrounding area. Within three months, 4,000 people were working in the diggings.

"The world came flocking in," wrote California historian Hubert Bancroft. "The region round Marshall's mill swarmed with gold seekers. Two thousand diggers were at work there with knives, picks, shovels, sticks, tin pans, wooden bowls, willow baskets and cradles...scraping rocky beds, riddling gravelly sand and washing dirt for the metal." It was said that in the process of "washing out the gold," the valley floor was lowered twenty feet.

In November 1848, Governor Richard Mason's

Henry, Sondra

Everyone Wears His Name :
A Biography of Levi Strauss

messenger arrived in Washington with gold dust worth $3,000. Then on December 5, 1848, President James Polk officially announced the location of the gold sources on the American River in California. This began yet another rush for riches.

Teachers, farmers, shopkeepers, blacksmiths, carpenters, and sailors got "gold fever." Lured by exaggerated stories of shoveling gold into sacks and finding mountains of solid gold, young men came to California from all over the United States and from all the countries of the world.

Of the 20,000 adventurers who began the trip to California in 1849, it is estimated that about 750 died. Many others arrived so ill from the long journey by sea or overland that they never completely recovered. Close to half of the wagons and animals never reached their destination. About 9,000 other hopeful miners came north from Mexico, or east from China and other Asian lands.

It was not unusual for the people of a town to pay for outfitting one or two of their young men and for their travel expenses to California. In return, the men would agree to share with their backers any gold they found.

A "forty-niner," as each of these gold seekers was called, needed about $750 to outfit himself. He required a tent and sleeping bag, tarpaulins, camp

equipment, and clothing. Then there were the necessary picks, shovels, and sledges for the actual digging. Medical supplies such as cholera pills were vital. In spite of careful preparation, many miners died of hardships during their search for gold.

The method of mining in the California gold fields was called placer mining, or panning. The miner used a pan or basin with round ridges on the bottom. He put several handfuls of dirt, along with some water, in his pan. With a few circular motions, the quartz, sand, and lightweight minerals washed over the side. After many washings, only gold and the heavy minerals remained.

If the gold particles were large enough, miners could easily separate the gold from the dirt and minerals. If not, other equipment was sometimes used. Either way, the work was hard and tedious and often yielded nothing.

Wherever gold was found, small mining towns soon appeared. The names of some of the towns—Hangman's Bridge, Hell's Half Acre, Jackass Hill, Devil's Nose, and Bedbug—reflect the hardships and trying times of the forty-niners. Gradually, businesspeople moved in to service the miners. Shops and offices opened, families came, and schools and churches were built.

These small mining towns depended on the

larger ones, such as San Francisco and Sacramento, to provide them with necessary supplies. Sometimes an occasional peddler would come through the mountains with goods for sale. More often, the miners—mostly single men who lived alone, or in camps with other men—would take a much-needed break from their hard work and travel to the city. Here they could spend some of their gold on supplies and entertainment. Sometimes, after becoming more established, miners or shopkeepers would go to San Francisco looking for brides to take back to the northern territories. In this way, gold helped many cities and towns in California grow.

As the forty-niners passed through San Francisco on their way to the mining sites, goods became scarcer and overpriced. Land values increased rapidly. San Francisco soon became a wild west city with a population of 50,000. Its harbor, a quiet cove only a few years before, welcomed thousands of men and women who had made the long ocean voyage to California, where they hoped to find a fortune in gold.

It is estimated that between 1848 and 1855, the forty-niners uncovered about $370 million of gold, or $41 million a year for nine years. However, most individuals who came looking for gold did not make their fortunes in the mines. The average miner

earned a total of $750. One historian claimed that 99 percent of the forty-niners would have done better if they had never left their "plowing and peddling and preaching."

Besides the few who did find wealth in gold, others made fortunes in real estate or by supplying the miners with pants, dry goods, and other needed items. Levi Strauss was one of these enterprising businesspeople. In this way, many became rich from the gold rush without discovering gold.

John Sutter himself never made a fortune. Although he profited at first from sales to the miners, this situation did not last long. Soon the miners, angered by the high prices they had to pay, began to steal what they needed. They overran Sutter's property, destroying what he had built, and paid nothing for their mining claims.

Sutter traveled east to Washington, D.C., to ask members of the U.S. Congress to pay him for the land he had lost to the miners. The appeal was denied on the grounds that the Swiss immigrant was actually a Mexican citizen. Since his grant from Mexico was not recognized by the United States, the U.S. government took control of his land along with the rest of California.

Sutter, whose wife and children had rejoined him in America, now settled in Pennsylvania. With

almost no funds, he continued to petition the U.S. government for payment. Finally, he did receive a small pension from the state of California, but neither he nor his family ever returned there. John Sutter died in 1880, poor and forgotten.

James Marshall, the first to find gold, did not benefit either. He did some prospecting on his own, and then worked in a variety of jobs. Marshall became increasingly bitter and angry. He died in 1885, disappointed and penniless.

Sam Brannon, the man who had helped start the gold rush, became a millionaire. He made his fortune, as he had hoped, through the business created by the thousands of forty-niners.

Gradually, the supply of California gold, never very large to begin with, no longer attracted many miners. People in other places discovered gold, luring adventurous miners with new promises of riches. By 1859, when silver was found in the Comstock Lode of the Nevada Territory, the wild and glorious California gold rush had ended. San Francisco had grown from a frontier town to a bustling city, and California had become one of the fastest growing states in the Union.

Selected Bibliography

"Annuals of Business: Bluejeans and Levi Strauss." *New Yorker*, Nov. 12, 1979.

"A Billion Levi's Later." *Politics Today*, July 1978.

Bloch, Jean Libman. "Blue Jean Revolution." *Saturday Evening Post*, Aug.-Sept., 1974.

Cogan, Sara G. *The Jews of San Francisco and the Greater Bay Area, 1849, 1919. An annotated bibliography.* Berkeley, California: Western Jewish History Center, 1973.

Cray, Ed. *Levi's*. Boston: Houghton, Mifflin, 1978.

Daily Alta California (San Francisco, California). Numerous articles from 1850 to 1902.

Dimont, Max. *The Jews in America: The Roots and Destiny of American Jews.* New York: Simon & Schuster, 1978.

"A Fifth Generation Levi's Chief." *Business Week*, Dec. 5, 1983.

Gordon, Thomas, and Max Morgan Witts. *The San Francisco Earthquake.* New York: Stein & Day, 1971.

Harris, Leon. *Merchant Princes: An Intimate History of Jewish Families Who Built Great Department Stores.* New York: Harper & Row, 1977.

"The Jeaning of America—and the World." *American Heritage*, April 1978.

Latchkin, Roger W. *San Francisco 1846-1856: From Hamlet to City.* New York: Oxford University Press, 1974.

"Levi Experiment." *Time*, March 20, 1972.

Levinson, Robert E. *The Jews in the California Gold Rush.* Berkeley, California: K'tav Publishing and Judah L. Magnes Memorial Museum, 1978.

"Levi Strauss Wants to be a Family Affair Again." *Business Week*, July 29, 1985.

Levy, Harriet Lane. *920 O'Farrell Street.* New York: Doubleday, 1947.

Lewis, Oscar. *This Was San Francisco: Being First-Hand Accounts of the Evolution of One of America's Favorite Cities.* New York: David McKay, 1962.

Lowenthal, M. *The Jews of Germany.* New York: Longman's, 1936.

Narell, Irena. *Our City: The Jews of San Francisco.* San Diego: Howell-North Books, 1981.

The Old West: The Forty Niners. New York: Time-Life Books, 1974.

"Return to the Basics Keeps Levi's Number One." *Business Week*, Jan. 19, 1976.

Rochlin, Harriet. *Pioneer Jews: New Life in the Far West.* Boston: Houghton, Mifflin, 1984.

Rosenbaum, Fred. *Architects of Reform: Congregational and Community Leadership of Temple Emanu-el of San Francisco, 1849-1980.* Berkeley, California: Judah L. Magnes Memorial Museum, 1980.

Roth, Art. "The Levi's Story." *American Heritage,* Fall 1952.

San Francisco Chronicle. Numerous articles, 1875-1902.

Schappes, Morris. *A Documentary History of the Jews in the United States.* New York: Schocken Books, 1950.

Schoener, Allon. *The American Jewish Album: 1654 to the Present.* New York: Rizzoli, 1983.

Stern, Norton, and William M. Kramer. "Levi Strauss, The Man Behind the Myth." *Western States Jewish History Quarterly,* April 1987.

"Those Pants That Levi Gave us: From Workmen's Duds to Jet-Set Chic." *American West,* July-Aug. 1985.

Wise, Isaac Meyer. *The Western Journal of Isaac Meyer Wise, 1877.* Ed. by Dr. William M. Kramer. Berkeley, California: Western Jewish History Center, 1974.

Index

anti-Semitism, 9, 31, 42
Bavaria, 7, 8, 9
blue jeans, 5, 7, 47, 108
Brando, Marlon, 109
California: Chinese in, 40, 66; Civil War and, 49, 50, 51; the gold rush and, 22; journeying to, 23-24; lifestyle in, 41; under Mexican rule, 27; people of, 31; the railroad and, 49; towns in, 38, 40
Carter, Jimmy, 112
Chinatown, 66
Civil War, 45, 49, 50-51
Daily Alta California, 53
Davis, Jacob: businesses of, 59; as a customer of Levi Strauss & Co., 58; at Levi Strauss & Co., 64, 77, 85; retirement of, 105; riveted pants and, 60-62, 63, 65
Davis, Simon, 105, 106
Dean, James, 109
denim, 37, 47
Eureka Benevolent Society, 55, 93
501 Double X Denim, 69, 86, 89, 107, 108, 109
"gold fever," 26
gold rush, the: the discovery of gold and, 22, 27; gold digging and, 38; gold seekers and, 23-24, 27, 33; mining camps during, 38; profit from, 51; supplies for, 36-37, 40
Great Depression, 106
Haas, Peter, 109
Haas, Robert D., 112
Haas, Walter, 105, 106, 107-108, 109
Haas, Walter, Jr., 109, 111

Hearst, William Randolph, 90
Hotel Del Monte, 97
Jews: attacks against, 9; beliefs of, 18, 21; in California, 31, 32, 42, 43, 44; The Civil War and, 49-50; in Germany, 7, 8; during the gold rush, 24, 26; holidays of, 57; immigration to the U.S. by, 10; in New York City, 15, 16
Jewish Quarter, 8
Kentucky, 18, 19, 21, 23
Koshland, Davis, 106, 109
landsmen, 15
Levi's: in the American West, 6; invention of, 60-61; origin of the name of, 108; popularity of, 111-112; as a symbol, 110; teenagers and, 110; trademark of, 85-86, 108
Levi's Plaza, 112
Levi Strauss & Co.: business policies of, 68, 88, 105, 108, 110; during the Civil War, 50-51; earthquakes and, 53-54, 102-103, 104; economic problems of, 104, 106; factories owned by, 65; formation of, 6; growth of, 73, 91, 95, 109; merchandise sold by, 44, 47, 64, 69, 84, 88-89, 106, 107-108; reputation of, 85; stock of, 111, 112; stores owned by, 52-53, 54; trademarks of, 6, 69
New York City, 12, 14, 15, 16, 102
Pacific Hebrew Orphan Asylum, 93
Paris, France, 85
peddlers, 18-19, 21, 38
Pony Express, 48-49
railroads: the Central Pacific, 58, 89;

changes caused by, 88; importance of, 49; the Pony Express and, 49; price fixing by, in California, 89; the Union Pacific and, 58, 89

Rebel Without a Cause, 109

Sahlein, Mary (half sister), 7, 9, 10, 17, 74

Sahlein, William (brother-in-law), 17, 45, 52, 74

Saint Francis Hotel, 78

San Francisco: Chinese in, 66-68; during the Civil War, 50; cultural events in, 57; earthquakes in, 52-53, 83, 102-103, 104; fires in, 52, 83; during the gold rush, 26-29, 33, 34; growth of, 29, 41, 51, 81; Jews in, 43, 44; "lawlessness" in, 41-42; newspapers in, 79, 90, 99; waterfront of, 32-33; women in, 41, 43; as Yerba Buena, 27

Spreckles, Claus, 90, 91

Stern, Abraham (nephew), 55, 73, 91, 100, 102-105

Stern, David (brother-in-law): children of, 54; death of, 72; first business of, 29, 31, 32; during the gold rush, 24, 40; home life of, 54; at Levi Strauss & Co., 35, 36, 45; marriage of, 17; relationship with Levi Strauss of, 40; religion of, 43

Stern, Fanny (sister): children of, 44, 54, 55; death of, 83; in Germany, 7, 9; during the gold rush, 24, 26; immigration to America by, 10; marriages of, 16-17, 74

Stern, Jacob (nephew): activities of, 104-105; early job of, 73; inheritance of, 100; at Levi Strauss & Co., 74, 85, 91, 95, 102; marriage of, 83;

relationship with Levi Strauss of, 44, 55, 57, 93; retirement of, 105

Stern, Louis (nephew), 55, 73, 91, 100, 102

Stern, Sigmund (nephew): children of, 96; inheritance of, 100; at Levi Strauss & Co., 85, 91, 95, 105; marriage of, 92; relationship with Levi Strauss of, 55, 78; retirement of, 106

Strauss, Jonas (half brother), 7, 9, 16, 17, 18, 45, 53

Strauss, Levi: appearance of, 29, 43, 54, 81; childhood of, 5, 7, 9; death of, 98; donations made by, 55, 80, 93, 96, 100; early businesses of, 32, 34, 36, 37, 45; funeral of, 98-100; during the gold rush, 29-30, 31, 37-38, 40; health of, 95-96; homes of, 54, 73, 75, 92; immigration to America by, 10-12; investments made by, 89-91; journey to California of, 26; in Kentucky, 18, 21; legends about, 6-7, 30; life-style of, 35, 41, 44, 57, 58, 71, 75-76, 77, 78, 92, 93, 97; in New York, 12, 14-16, 18, 19; as a peddler, 5, 21, 48; railroads and, 89-91; religion of, 43; reputation of, 40, 54-55, 79

Strauss, Louis (half brother), 7, 9, 16, 18, 45, 74, 83

Strauss, Nathan (nephew), 45, 75, 78

Sutter's Mill, 22

Temple Emanu-el, 43, 55, 57, 67, 99, 102

"Two Horse Brand," 86

University of California, 95, 105

Vietnam War, 110

The Wild Ones, 109

World War II, 108